D1742288

# CAREER PILOT BLUEPRINT

## How to Become & _Succeed_ as a Professional Pilot

Gregory Youngs

Career Pilot Blueprint

Copyright © 2014

Gregory Youngs

All rights reserved.

# DEDICATION

This book is dedicated to the most important people in my life.
Dawn, Connor and Morgan.

Career Pilot Blueprint

# CONTENTS

|  | Introduction | 7 |
|---|---|---|
| 1 | Industry outlook | 9 |
| 2 | So You Want To Be A professional Pilot? | 11 |
| 3 | Getting Qualified | 13 |
| 4 | How To Get Your Ratings As Fast & Affordably As Possible | 23 |
| 5 | How To Ace Your Checkrides | 28 |
| 6 | Your Personal Career Blueprint | 33 |
| 7 | Entry Level Jobs | 35 |
| 8 | Career Options | 39 |
| 9 | Time Building | 49 |
| 10 | The Job Hunt | 55 |
| 11 | Your Resume | 66 |
| 12 | Mastering The Art of the Interview | 75 |
| 13 | Financing the Dream | 89 |
| 14 | Specific Rating Requirements | 97 |
| 15 | Pilot Pay Rates | 122 |
| 16 | College Aviation Programs | 126 |
| 17 | Flight School Directory | 132 |

Career Pilot Blueprint

# INTRODUCTION

"When once you have tasted flight, you will forever walk the earth with your eyes turned skyward, for there you have been, and there you will always long to return." – Leonardo da Vinci

## Introduction

Congratulations. If you are reading this, you are no doubt seriously interested in a career as a professional pilot, or in taking your pilot career to the next level. The information contained in this program will guide you step-by-step from where you are now to a paid position in the cockpit. Perhaps you have zero flight time and a dream. Or you may be a low time pilot looking for the smartest ways to climb the aviation career ladder. Either way, you will find this information to be extremely helpful. I was able to achieve my goal of becoming a professional pilot, and can help you do the same. Deciding to pursue a career as a pilot is not one to be taken lightly. Earning the ratings and experience you will need for even an entry-level pilot job will require hard work, time and money. The early part of your career is likely to consist of both long hours and low pay. But, as your experience grows so will the opportunities available to you. If you're like I was at the beginning of my career, you are starting with little more than a dream. I did not have the privilege of being accepted into the military flight training program. I had not yet completed my four year degree. I did not have the money I would need to pay for my ratings. I did not have any "connections" in the aviation industry to seek advice from. All I had was a dream and a passionate commitment to turn it into a reality. I obtained my ratings, towed gliders and banners, flew charters in the Bahamas, flew crop dusters, flew turboprops and jets for an airline, and landed a corporate captain flying job. It has been a fantastic adventure. Not always easy, but always rewarding. There were many hard earned lessons along the way. Lessons I can now share with you to accelerate you along your career path. I am honored to be your "connection" in the aviation industry. And it is my goal to provide you with the real world information you need transform *your* dream from a "wish" into a tangible and achievable plan of action. As you go through life many things will catch your eye, but only a few will catch your heart. Only a few will become a true passion. Those are the ones worth pursuing. Are you *passionate* about flying? You will be spending a major portion of your life working. Why wouldn't you want to make your passion and your profession one and the same? I've had grand adventures, been witness to scenes more beautiful than you can imagine and worked with many great people. And now more than 30 years after my first solo, I still find myself looking up each time I hear a plane flying over. If it's your desire to become a professional pilot, let me be the first to welcome you on this rewarding path. Let's get going!

# CHAPTER 1

## THE INDUSTRY OUTLOOK

## The Industry Outlook

Like every industry, aviation is cyclical and directly impacted by the overall economy. The economic crisis of 2008 precipitated several sluggish years of hiring by the airlines as well as corporate flight departments. But the demand for pilots is now improving measurably. It is predicted that the airline industry is about to embark on the biggest surge of pilot hiring in its history. A forecast by Boeing Aircraft indicates that there will be a worldwide demand for **466,650 additional commercial pilots by 2029**. And they are not alone. FlightSafety International also projects a demand for **500,000 pilots over the next 20 years**. That averages more than 23,000 new pilots each year. The strong demand for qualified pilots could well result in an industry shortage. Airlines in Asia and the Middle East are actively recruiting pilots from America and other countries. The market for qualified commercial pilots is rapidly becoming a global one. This is excellent news for those in the beginning stages of their pilot careers. The opportunities for employment are no longer just "domestic". There are real and growing opportunities to fly for airlines from around the globe. This dramatic growth in hiring will be driven by multiple factors, including:

- A significant number of airline pilots are reaching mandatory retirement age. Large numbers of pilots will need to be hired simply to maintain the current staffing levels.
- Recent changes to pilot work rules have increased pilot rest requirements and will necessitate an incremental increase in pilot employment.
- As the US and global economies rise, there will be a commensurate increase in demand for air travel.
- Emerging economies in Asia and elsewhere are seeing a boom in air travel, both airline and corporate. It is predicted that Asia will soon become the number one market for air travel in the world.
- The military is not training as many pilots as in previous decades. They are also retaining pilots for a longer period of time than in years past.

Keep in mind that the airlines aren't the only ones able to offer great flying jobs. Corporate, charter, fractional and government flying jobs will all see increased hiring thanks to an improving economy and the absorption of qualified candidates by the airlines. There are many attractive career options for pilots outside of the airlines. We will review many of those in detail.

# CHAPTER 2

## SO YOU WANT TO BE A PROFESSIONAL PILOT?

## So You Want to Be a Professional Pilot?

**The Upside.** Being a professional pilot is easily one of the most rewarding and interesting careers you could choose. A captain for a major airline earns an average salary of $150,000 per year while working approximately of 14 days per month. Airline pilots typically have the ability to "commute" at no cost. This means that while you may be *based* in Newark, you could choose to *live* in South Florida. A pilot with many airlines can expect their lifetime earnings to total in the *millions*. Corporate pilots can have an equally enviable income and lifestyle. Flying is also a career with a certain amount of prestige associated with it. When asked, you will be proud to tell people that you are a captain for ABC airlines, or fly a Learjet for XYZ Corp. Your work will be occasionally challenging, often fun and always rewarding. You will have the opportunity go places and see things that most people can only dream about. There have been many occasions that I have looked down through that jet cockpit window and thought about all the people who are stuck in jobs they can't stand. And here I am, actually getting paid to live my dream and fly multimillion dollar jets around the country.

**The Downside.** It will take time, money and hard work to earn the qualifications needed for a commercial flying job. Your first flying jobs are not likely to be very lucrative. You will be required to maintain good health and be able to pass a medical exam every 6 to 12 months. If you fail you will be grounded, at least until you can correct the issue. If you work for an airline you will also be required to successfully pass initial training, both ground school and simulator. There will be regular recurrent training, and check rides as you upgrade or move from one aircraft type to another. There are few professionals who are scrutinized as closely as pilots. This is no doubt a major reason why commercial aviation has such a remarkable safety record. Also, it goes without saying that for many pilots, the job entails a good deal of time away from home. This is a lifestyle not everyone enjoys. You will need to decide for yourself.

That said, if a career as a professional pilot is your objective, don't let the hurdles intimidate you. Trust me when I say it *is* possible and *you can* do it. Remember, obstacles are what you see when you take your eye off of your goal. No amount of money can "buy" you a successful aviation career if you have a poor work ethic and a bad attitude. But if you are willing to work hard, have a professional attitude and the dedication to do whatever it takes to achieve your dream there is little that can stop you.

# CHAPTER 3

## GETTING QUALIFIED

## Getting Qualified

What are the qualifications required to be a professional pilot? Typically, a professional pilot is going to hold at least a commercial, multiengine and instrument rating. The absolute *minimum* qualifications you will need in order to get paid for work as a pilot would be a commercial pilot certificate. It is possible to obtain a private pilot license and then a commercial certificate without obtaining an instrument rating. This would result in a "limited" commercial certificate. The pilot would be restricted to flights in VFR weather (visual flight rules), in a single-engine airplane and within a 50 mile radius of his departure airport if he is carrying passengers. This basic level of commercial certification opens the door to a few types of flying jobs. These could include towing gliders, towing banners, sightseeing flights and agricultural aviation. However, I would *strongly encourage* you to obtain your instrument rating *prior* to obtaining your commercial rating and looking for a job. Remember, having limited qualifications equals having limited opportunity.

Pilots will generally obtain their ratings in the following order:

- Student Pilot
- Private Pilot*
- Instrument Rating

- Commercial (Requires 195 to 250 hours of flight experience)
- Multiengine**
- Certified Flight Instructor (CFI)
- Airline Transport Pilot (ATP, requires 1500 hours of flight experience)

* The Recreational and Sport Pilot Certificates have been omitted as they are not the best stepping stones toward advanced ratings.

** Prior to or after obtaining a multiengine rating, some pilots will obtain one or more Certified Flight Instructor (CFI) ratings. In addition to the basic CFI, there is the CFII or "Certified Flight Instructor Instrument" which allows you to teach instrument flying and the MEI or multiengine instructor rating. Obtaining flight instructor ratings is by no means required for pilots who have no intention of working as flight instructors. If you have other opportunities to build flight time, then the money which you would have otherwise invested in flight instructor ratings could be invested in building a multi-engine flight time or other training as dictated by your particular circumstance.

After earning the appropriate ratings *some* entry-level flying jobs will be within your reach. These will be "time building" jobs such as flight instructing, banner towing, traffic patrol, etc. The next step up will be a charter, corporate or regional airline job. Although there are no hard and fast rules with regard to charter and corporate jobs, regional airlines will require a minimum of 1500 hours total time and 50 to 100 hours of multi-engine time due to the recently enacted rule requiring that airline first officers meet the requirements to hold an ATP rating. A reduction in the 1500 hour rule is available for military pilots and pilots graduating from approved university programs.

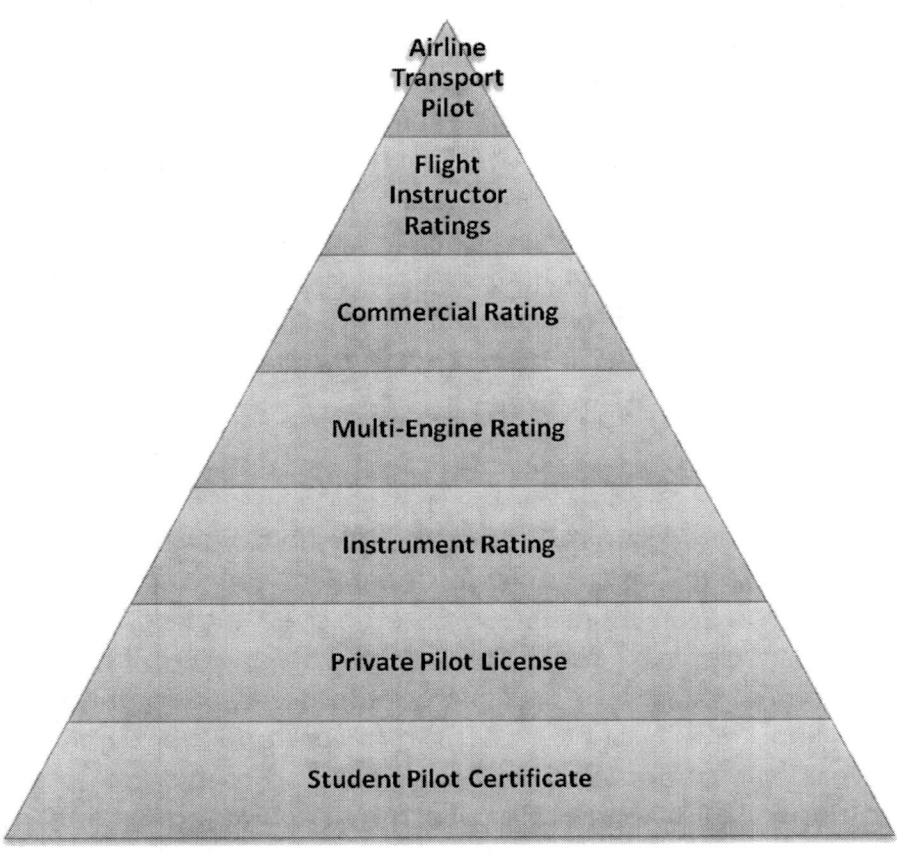

Airline
Transport
Pilot

Flight
Instructor
Ratings

Commercial Rating

Multi-Engine Rating

Instrument Rating

Private Pilot License

Student Pilot Certificate

## Typical Pilot Progression

## Medical Certificates

Pilots are required to pass a physical examination administered by a doctor who is an FAA-authorized aviation medical examiner. There are three classes of medical certificate, first-class, second-class and third-class. A first or second class medical is required for commercial pilots. A third-class certificate is sufficient for student and private pilots. I would encourage you to obtain a first-class medical right away. If there are any health issues that need to be addressed in order for you to obtain a first class medical, you want to know about it sooner rather than later. Don't be afraid of the medical examiner. If you do have an issue they can be very helpful in assisting you to correct the problem or potentially obtain a waiver.

## College Degrees

Is a college degree mandatory? The short answer is no. You don't have to have a college degree to work as professional pilot. However, there are some employers that do require a four-year degree. Remember, when you apply for flying jobs there are going to be multiple candidates vying for the same position. You want to be as qualified and competitive a candidate as possible. The fact is that most major airline and *at least* half of corporate pilots have a college degree. It really does not matter what school you choose to attend or what you major in. All other things being equal, the pilot with the degree is going to have the edge on the pilot who does not. Also, don't think that you *must* major in an aviation related field. In fact, I would encourage you to consider earning a degree in an *unrelated* field. I have flown with pilots who were educated to be lawyers, pharmacists, accountants, etc. and they were far less worried about being laid off or furloughed than the pilots who had no other experience or skill set to fall back on. A good pilot always has a plan B. That said, there are a number of community colleges offering two-year associate degrees in aviation. This could be a great way to earn some college credit and possibly earn your initial ratings with the help of a low interest student loan. You could then transfer to a four-year college to complete your bachelor's degree either on campus or online. See chapter 16 for directory of colleges offering aviation related degrees and pilot training programs.

## Age

In decades past it was much harder for pilots getting a "late start" to have hope of landing a job at an airline. Fortunately, that is not the case today. Pilots are being hired by both regional and major airlines well into their 50s. With a mandatory retirement age of 65 for airlines, your career will be shorter than for others. But if you are in good health, there is absolutely no reason not to go for it. Don't let the kids have all the fun!

## Choosing a Flight School

Choosing the right flight school(s) is very important. Training costs can vary considerably between flight schools. So can the quality of the equipment and instructors. Don't be seduced by the big flight schools glossy brochures and flashy websites. Conversely, don't pick  a school simply because they are cheaper. Things to consider...

1. **Reputation**. If possible, speak to current and former students. What kind of experience did they have? Did the school deliver as advertised? Are they asking you to pay significant amounts of money up front? I would discourage you from paying significant amounts of money in advance to *any* flight school. While that may be safe with large established schools like American Flyers, Embry Riddle, Flight Safety or ATP, be cautious with newer small schools. More than one flight school has shut down before delivering all the training the students have paid for. I would recommend that you "pay-as-you-go" at a smaller school.

2. **Experienced instructors**. A good instructor will provide you with a solid foundation of skills and education to build on and will help you obtain your rating(s) in the most efficient manner possible. You'll want to make sure that your instructor has the availability to fly with you with sufficient frequency. If you want to train full-time, don't pick a part-time instructor or one who already has a full schedule. Most of the larger flight schools do an excellent job of training their instructors and are able to keep their students progressing quickly toward their ratings.

3. **A quality fleet**. Does the flight school have enough airplanes to meet the demand of the students? Are the aircraft well maintained? Are the aircraft well equipped with modern avionics, GPS, etc.? Do they have a multi-engine aircraft? Do they have an instrument simulator available for your use?

4. **Glass panel vs. Analog panel?** Over the past decade a revolution has taken place in light aircraft avionics. The traditional analog or "steam gauges" as they are

often referred to, are being rapidly replaced with "glass panel" technology. A glass panel has become standard equipment in virtually all new aircraft being produced today. There is no question that a glass panel will be in your future as a professional pilot. So, does this mean that you should only train at a flight school with glass panel equipped aircraft? No, this should not be a deciding factor. You will definitely want to build some experience in glass paneled aircraft in the course of your training, but it is not essential that you earn your private license in this type of aircraft. In fact, a strong case could be made for the benefits of learning in an analog equipped aircraft. Keep in mind that the majority of the aircraft in service around the world are still analog equipped. To be well prepared for the "real world", you will want exposure to and experience with both types of equipment.

5. **Controlled or uncontrolled airport?** There are essentially two types of airports, controlled and uncontrolled. An uncontrolled airport does not have a control tower and utilizes a "unicom" frequency which pilots use to announce their position and intentions to one another. A controlled airport will have a control  tower directing aircraft and clearing them for takeoffs, departures and ground operations. Students who train at a controlled airport quickly become accustomed to obtaining clearances and communicating with the controllers. As a professional pilot this is something

you're going to be doing day in and day out. The sooner you become comfortable in this environment the better. One consideration is that when flying out of a busy controlled airport you're going to be paying more in aircraft rental time sitting on the ground waiting for clearances, waiting to taxi and waiting to take off. A good balance would be a controlled airport with lighter traffic. There are many controller airports that have little or no airline traffic. All other things being equal, these can make a great location for your initial training. This should not be the determining factor in selecting a flight school, but should be taken into consideration.

6. Part 61 vs. part 141. Basically, flight schools operate under one of two sets of FAA guidelines, "Part 61" or "Part 141". A Part 141 program has a curriculum approved by the FAA which must be followed closely. Because of this rigid structure they are by necessity less flexible than a Part 61 program.

# Part 61 vs. Part 141

|  | Part 61 | Part 141 |
|---|---|---|
| Curriculum | May vary depending on the needs of the student. | A predetermined syllabus is used for all students. |
| Difficulty | Students train to proficiency. | Students are tested in "stage checks" which must be passed to move to the next phase. |
| Flexibility | Curriculum can be adjusted as the student and instructor desire. | Follows a set curriculum in a step by step format. |
| Accelerated Training | Yes if coordinated by instructor(s) and dependent on the students ability. | Yes.  Accelerated training programs are normally available. |
| Ground School | Ground training with your CFI and or self study. | In classroom study with written tests. |
| Testing | FAA written test and FAA checkride. | Additional written tests and stage checks. |
| Cost | Typically less expensive. | Typically more expensive. |
| Financing | Available. | Available.  VA benefits may only be used at a Part 141 school. |

So which is better? The truth is that neither is "better". In part, it comes down to your circumstances and personal preference. Some students, particularly those training on a part-time or sporadic basis may benefit from the flexibility of a Part 61 training program. A significant benefit of a Part 141 program is the ability to earn your ratings with fewer flight hours. You can earn your private license in 35 flight hours versus 40, and your commercial certificate in 190 flight hours versus 250. If you'll be training full time (or close to it) you should be able to obtain your ratings in fewer flight hours in a Part 141 program. Theoretically, this could reduce the time you spend in flight school by weeks or even months. While this will not always translate into a cost savings, there is a real advantage to becoming qualified to enter the job market as soon as possible. Many students benefit from a more rigid structure of a Part 141 program. The clearly defined syllabus keeps students on track and helps students take the most efficient route to obtaining their ratings. Some of the larger flight schools offer to hire graduates of their career pilot programs as flight instructors. For some, this could be a significant benefit.

Do your homework and check out several flight schools before making a commitment. You will need to weigh the variables of cost, time frame, equipment, geography, etc. and choose the one that you feel will best help you achieve your specific goals.

# CHAPTER 4

# HOW TO GET YOUR RATINGS AS FAST AND *AFFORDABLY* AS POSSIBLE.

## How to get your ratings as *fast* and *affordably* as possible.

Since your goal is to become a professional pilot, you will need to approach your training with a professional attitude. You certainly want to have fun and enjoy the process. But you are on a mission. Your mission is to earn the qualifications to become a professional pilot. And you want to do it in the most efficient and cost-effective manner possible. Keep the following points in mind.

- **Have a plan.** If your flight school or instructor have not clearly laid out a step-by-step plan to get you from where you are now to the rating(s) you are after, insist that they do so. Without a well structured curriculum, students and instructors may tend to "drift", and work haphazardly toward your goal. Remember the mission, don't waste time and money.

- **Know the requirements.** This sounds obvious but it's critical that you know *exactly* what is required to qualify for the particular rating you're working on. This will keep you from wasting time and money exceeding one requirement while neglecting another. Track your progress on paper. This is particularly important if you're training in a Part 61 flight school.

- **Be prepared.** Enroll in a ground school course as soon as possible. You can even do this before you start flying. Preparing for and passing your private pilot written test early will help to shorten your total training time. When you are paying *well* over $100 an hour for flight training, you don't want your instructor to be spending a lot of time teaching you what you should have already learned on the ground. In addition to the ground school you receive from your instructor, consider attending one of the accelerated test prep courses. These typically involve two days of intense classroom preparation and end with you taking the actual FAA written test. Most students are able to pass with a fairly high score. I used this method to help prepare for my private, commercial and ATP written tests. My lowest score was 94. I used both American Flyers and ATP and had a good experience with each. There are also some great resources available in the form of DVD and online courses. King Schools, Sporty's and American Flyers are sources I recommend. A DVD is a great resource because you can repeat a topic you're having difficulty with as many times as it takes. After you receive the necessary flight training toward your private pilots license you will take a check ride with an FAA designated examiner. He will administer both an oral exam and a flight test. You are required to provide him with a copy of your written test results. A high score on your written test indicates that you've studied and "know your stuff". A barely passing score could result in a lengthier and more difficult oral exam that focuses on your weak areas. In short, study hard and get as high a score as possible on your written test!

- **Don't waste money on gadgets.** We all like cool toys, but for now save your money. Buy only the things that you actually *need*. You don't *need* a $900 Bose noise canceling headset. You don't *need* a $300 flight bag. You don't *need* $1500 handheld GPS. What you *need* is to learn as much as possible. Only invest in things that move you closer to your goal of becoming a professional pilot. Remember the mission!

- **Dump your instructor.** If you don't feel that you and your instructor are compatible or you have a serious personality conflict, ask for a new one. You will be working very closely with your instructor and it is important that you have a good working relationship. Also, I've seen instructors who are simply burned out and are just going through the motions. There are occasionally instructors who will "milk" students by flying more hours than may be necessary in order to pad their own wallet and logbook. Fortunately, these are the rare exception. You will find most flight instructors to be thoroughly professional. But if you do get a weak one, or simply can't get along with your instructor don't hesitate to politely ask for a change.

- **Play games!** For around $30 you can buy Microsoft Flight Simulator for your computer. If you are a Mac user you can purchase X-Plane. While these are "technically"

games, you can learn a great deal while having fun. The instruments and controls are remarkably accurate. The navigation radios and GPS work just like the real thing. It is fun with a purpose.

- **Simulate.** A certain number of training hours conducted in an approved simulator can be credited toward your various rating requirements. The hourly rate for time in a flight simulator is usually considerably lower than for an actual aircraft. In the initial stages of my training I was not interested in simulators. I wanted to fly the "real thing". It was not until later as a professional pilot that I learned the real value of simulator training. Don't feel like the simulator is something *less* than the airplane. It is a very efficient and effective learning tool. I encourage you to take full advantage of this type of training if available. In addition, there are some excellent IFR simulation programs for your PC. While you will not be able to log this time, it will help you sharpen your skills and knowledge when working on your instrument rating.

- **Read.** In addition to your training materials and manuals, I would encourage you to read aviation magazines as well. *Flying, Private Pilot, AOPA, Flight Training* and others are a great resource. They will keep you abreast of the current industry news and are full of pilot reports and technical articles that will improve your aviation knowledge. In aviation, the leaders are readers.

Listen & Learn!

- **Listen.** Ask for advice. When you meet experienced pilots and flight instructors, don't be shy about asking for their advice. Most pilots are more than willing to share what they have learned with aspiring pilots. It is highly likely that some of the instructors where you will be training will be actively seeking jobs with the regional airlines or other employers. They might be able to share their experiences in trying to move up the aviation ladder. The industry is always in flux and they may be able to provide you with the latest information on hiring minimums, etc. Listen to what they and others have to say. It is smart to learn from our own experience and mistakes. But it's even smarter to learn from the experience and mistakes of others.

- **Pick up the pace.** If you're not in the position to undertake your flight training on a full-time basis, I still encourage you to fly as frequently as your schedule and budget permit. Instructors will tell you that flying more often will allow you to earn your flight ratings with fewer training hours. Flying more than once a week allows the previous flight lesson to still be fresh in your mind. In the early stages of your flight training, extended intervals between flights will have you spending the first half of each lesson relearning and polishing skills from the prior lesson.

# CHAPTER 5

## HOW TO ACE YOUR CHECK RIDES

### How to Ace Your Check Rides

Each rating or certificate you obtain requires that you pass a check ride with an FAA examiner. Anticipation of this event causes many pilots an undue amount of stress and anxiety. You will hear rumors that examiners are required to fail X% of students. This is a myth and is absolutely untrue. The examiner is not going to try and "trick you" and is not out to see you fail. Nor is he going to fail you in order to meet some non-existent requirement to maintain a specific pass-fail ratio.

**The Practical Test Standards.** The fact is that all examiners have a set of rules which they must follow. And those rules are spelled out in the PTS or Practical Test Standards. Each rating has a corresponding PTS and it is a document that you should become intimately familiar with prior to your check ride. The examiner can only test you on items contained in the applicable PTS so there should be no surprises. Pay particular attention to "Special Emphasis Areas". The PTS states that they are "essential to flight safety and _will be_ evaluated during the practical test."

**Mock Check Ride.** If your instructor doesn't offer it to you, ask them to conduct at least one "practice check ride" for you. Your instructor may be familiar with the way the examiner conducts his check ride. They often have a typical pattern they use and repeat. This information can help you anticipate and better prepare for your actual check ride. Ask your instructor to make it as *realistic* as possible. The examiner won't be giving you tips on how to improve your maneuvers during the check ride. He will be observing and critiquing afterwards. Don't let your instructor "coach you through" the maneuvers. If you're going to make a mistake or have a weak point you want to find it and corrected *before* your exam.

**Be Organized**. Be sure that you have everything you need in the way of documents, equipment, etc. for the check ride. The PTS actually has a list of everything you will need to bring to the check ride.

**The Airplane**. Make sure that you are *very* familiar with the airplane you be taking a check ride in. You will want to use the airplane you're most familiar with for check ride. Be sure and schedule it well in advance. You don't want to show up on the appointed day only to find out the aircraft is down for a scheduled maintenance or away for any other reason. You don't want to take a check ride in an airplane with unfamiliar radios, GPS, etc. if you can help it.

**Ask the Examiner**. Most Examiners would be happy to answer questions about an upcoming check ride. If the examiner is routinely at your flight school, try and spend a few minutes with him and your instructor asking him what you should expect during your check ride. This will accomplish two things. One, they will very likely answer your question! And secondly, you'll have the opportunity to meet the examiner in a "no stress" scenario. When the check ride comes around the examiner won't be a stranger who you are meeting for the first time.

**The Oral Exam.** The best advice I can give you with regards to passing your oral exam is to do well on your written exam! The examiner will be provided with the results of your written test. There are codes in the results that will let the examiner know exactly what area or areas you were weak in. You can rest assured that the examiner will spend some time focusing on these areas to make sure that you are up to speed. If you have a chance to talk with other students who've taken a check ride with the same examiner, do so. They often have "favorite" questions or scenarios that they tend to repeat in oral exams. Knowing these in advance can be helpful.

**Written Test Results.** It is very important that you do well on each FAA written exam. It will demonstrate to the examiner that you have a solid grasp of the information related to that particular rating. A barely passing grade on the written exam is almost guaranteed to result in a lengthier oral exam. Conversely a student with a nearly perfect score is likely to have a shorter oral exam. There are numerous resources to assist you in doing well on your written exams. In addition to any ground school your flight school may offer there are numerous "test prep" courses available as well as computer-based training and test preparation courses. And remember, this is about more than just passing the test. As a professional pilot you want to be as knowledgeable and well informed as possible. As a professional you don't want to settle for just "passing". You want to excel.

**How a Check Ride Ends.** There are three possible outcomes for a check ride. 1. You passed! You will be given a temporary certificate and can legally exercise the privileges of your newly acquired rating. 2. The pink slip. The issuance of a pink slip means that you have failed the test. Although you have failed a particular task or maneuver, the examiner can allow you to demonstrate the remaining required tasks and maneuvers. In this instance, during your retest you only have to demonstrate those parts of the test that were unsatisfactory or not yet completed. 3. A Formal Discontinuance. There are several situations in which a discontinuance is acceptable. These would include mechanical issues with the aircraft, poor weather or illness. You'll have the opportunity to complete the portions of the flight test or oral exam that were left unfinished. Don't panic if you bust a check ride, it is not the end of the world. You will be required to get additional training related to the tasks you failed. The student will not have to take the *entire* check ride and oral exam again. Will a failed check ride hurt your job prospects? No. *Anyone*, even the sharpest pilot can fail a check ride. You certainly don't want develop a pattern of failing check ride after check ride. That would create a problem. But busting your initial private or instrument check ride is just a bump in the road that many successful professional pilots have experienced as well.

**Your Logbook**
Your pilot logbook not only tracks your flight time but documents your flight experience and qualifications for employment as a professional pilot. It is important that you keep your logbook neat and up-to-date. If your logbook is inaccurate or sloppy it will become an issue with FAA examiner's as well as employers who may review it during a job interview. Always double check your math and make sure that the totals are correct. If you do make an error in your log book, do not erase or white out any information. Simply make

a new entry correcting the mistake with an explanation in the comments section. Don't fudge your time! One of the flight schools where I flew had a pilot who was busted for falsifying his logbook. During the oral exam on his commercial check ride the examiner reviewed the pilots logbook to confirm that he had the appropriate experience. The examiner noticed that he had "logged" a good deal of multi-engine time. It turns out that the student had simply "penciled in" flight time in a locally based twin. Unfortunately for the student, the twin in question was owned by the examiner! The result? *All* of the pilots ratings were revoked. If he wanted to earn his ratings back he would have to *start from scratch*. In case you missed the rather obvious moral to the story, don't risk it! If you're using a paper-based logbook, make sure that you make copies at regular intervals and keep them in a safe place. As your experience grows it will be very difficult to reproduce these records in the event you lose your logbook. The same rule applies if you use a computer-based electronic logbook. Keep a printout in a safe place and have a digital backup as well.

# CHAPTER 6

# YOUR *PERSONAL* CAREER BLUEPRINT

Dream Job!

## Your *Personal* Career Blueprint.

Your professional career will consume a *major* portion of your life. Yet very few pilots take the time to *truly* plan their careers. Often, they take the first opportunity that comes along, only to quit and change jobs every time a "slightly" better job is available. Don't let your career be dictated by chance. I would encourage you to be **strategic** with regard to your career choices. Think beyond the short term to your ultimate goal(s). Remember, that a career is much more than just a paycheck. What is a nice paycheck *really* worth if you're never home to spend it, or hate your job? Further, your career choices should be very personal in nature. You are the one that has to live with them. Be sure that the dream you're pursuing is your own. Here are some things to consider.

- What is my ultimate "career" goal?
- What is my ultimate "lifestyle" goal?
- What is the ideal interim job(s) I would like to have?

- Will this job give me the "correct" kind of experience?
- What kind of flying do you *really* want to do?
- Where do you want to live?
- How much time off to you want to have?
- What kind of salary do you need?
- How will this short-term decision impact my long-term goals?

These are just a few of the things you should consider. I encourage you to add to this list. What is *your* dream job? Becoming a captain for Delta? Flying a Gulfstream V? Flying a seaplane in the islands? Whatever the answer, *your* dream job is out there. Your job is to *think from the end* and "reverse engineer" the career you desire. What experience, qualities and qualifications does the ideal candidate for *your* dream job possess? *That* is the person you want to become. *Those* are the qualifications and experience you want to gain as quickly as possible. Take out a piece of paper and write down your career goals. Give careful thought to how you want to go about achieving those goals. You don't have to know *exactly* how you're going to get there today. But it is important that you take the time to write out your career goals including the interim steps and qualifications needed. Taking the time to thoughtfully put it down on paper is the difference between having a daydream and having an actionable career plan to guide you. Without a clear destination, any route will look good.

# CHAPTER 7

## ENTRY LEVEL JOBS

### BUILDING EXPERIENCE

**Entry-Level Jobs**

Okay, so now you have earned your ratings and are a commercially rated pilot. Congratulations! The next step is to become an *employed* commercially rated pilot. Obviously, your first job is not going to be flying a heavy jet for a major airline. That can come later. Let's examine some of the entry-level flying jobs that a newly minted commercial pilot can realistically obtain.

**Flight Instructor**

A position as a flight instructor is frequently the first "professional" flying job for commercial pilots. Newly rated instructors are often able to obtain a position at the same flight school where they obtained their ratings. This makes perfect sense as the flight school management and other instructors have likely gotten to know you well through the course of your training. They will know firsthand about your level of skill as a pilot and know kind of person you would be like to work with on a day-to-day basis. Working in a busy flight school can give you the opportunity to accumulate flight time quickly. And it is a fact that the best way to learn something is to teach it. You will become very sharp with regard to the fundamentals. That said, unless you intend to be a career flight instructor, after a reasonable period of time building you will need to start preparing for the next step. If the flight school you work for offers multi-engine instruction, you're going to want to become one of the multiengine instructors as soon as possible. Building multi-engine time is going to be critical to becoming qualified for a job as a charter, corporate or airline pilot. One advantage of flight instructing will be your exposure to the "multi-pilot" environment. Most corporate and all airline jobs involve coordination between multiple crewmembers.

## Banner Tow Pilot

You've probably been on the beach or at a stadium and seen a plane fly slowly by pulling an advertising banner. You probably thought that it looked like fun. Well you are right, it is! And it is possible to build several hundred hours of pilot in command time over the course of a summer season. Like giving primary flight instruction, the flight time that you're building is primarily single-engine, daytime VFR. Frequently, Cessna 172's are used as tow planes. However, many operators fly Piper Super Cubs or other "taildragger" aircraft. Depending on the type of aircraft the operator uses, you may need to obtain a tail wheel endorsement which typically requires at least five hours of dual instruction. Learning how to master a taildragger will sharpen your piloting skills and give you an appreciation for your rudder that few pilots of tricycle gear aircraft will ever know. Banner tow operators generally provide training for newly hired pilots. Pay close attention during training, ask questions and make sure you're comfortable with all the required procedures. The nature of banner towing requires operating aircraft in close proximity to the ground for banner pickups as well as a good deal of "low and slow" flying. Having been a banner tow pilot for several hundred hours I don't consider this type of flying to be especially "dangerous" but there are inherent risks. If you go this route, I encourage you to be exceedingly safety conscious and maintain a professional approach to your flying.

## Glider Tow Pilot

Towing gliders can be another good opportunity to build flight time. Typically, glider pilots don't want to be towed any higher than necessary in order to catch some thermal activity and have a good flight. As a tow pilot you may log as many as a half a dozen takeoffs and landings per flight hour. There are glider operations in most parts of the country. An online search of the Soaring Society of America's website will lead you to a list of glider operations. www.ssa.org

## Jump Plane Pilot

A jump plane pilot is employed by a skydiving operation to transport the skydivers up to altitude for their jumps. A jump pilot can log quite a few hours at a busy operation. Many different types of aircraft are used. I've seen everything from a Cessna 182 all the way up to a DC-3. Some larger operations use twin engine turbine aircraft such as the Beechcraft King Air and the DeHavilland Twin Otter. Needless to say, the opportunity to build multiengine turbine time would be *extremely* valuable. You can locate skydiving operations at www.dropzone.com

## Traffic Watch Pilot

Local radio stations sometimes do live reporting of traffic conditions from light aircraft. The most common aircraft used are Cessna 152's and 172's. Typically radio stations will contract with a local FBO for the aircraft and pilots. While the pay is low, you may be able to log as many as four or five hours a day.

**Power Line or Pipeline Patrol**

Some low time pilots are able to secure jobs as power line or pipeline patrol pilots. These jobs entail flying over many miles of rural power lines or pipelines to inspect them for leaks, damage, etc. Often the pilot will be carrying a "spotter" who will be doing the visual inspections during the flight.

**Sightseeing Flights**

In many parts of the country, there are operators who offer sightseeing tours or "scenic flights". The typical aircraft used would be a Cessna 172 or similar light aircraft. Some operators fly open cockpit biplanes (which would require you to have tailwheel experience), and the largest aircraft include turboprop Twin Otters used for tours over the Grand Canyon by Grand Canyon Airlines and Scenic Airlines.

# CHAPTER 8

## CAREER OPTIONS

### Career Options

Aviation is a very diverse industry. It is not unusual for pilots to consider airline and corporate flying positions to be the "good jobs" and dismiss everything else as something other than that. I would encourage you to avoid this sort of limited thinking. Thousands of pilots choose to spend their entire career in lesser known but very rewarding corners of aviation. The fact is there is a lot of opportunity out there for pilots in addition to the airline and corporate world. Here are just a few of the many niches a pilot could consider.

## The Airlines

### Regional Airlines

The regional airline industry has evolved dramatically over the last two decades. In years past it was viewed as a place you went to "pay your dues" until you could land a job with a major airline. Most had a fleet comprised exclusively of small turboprops. Today the lines between the regional airlines and major airlines have blurred somewhat. A regional airline pilot can find himself flying and 90+ passenger jet. And while the regionals can't match the salaries that the major airlines pay, they have become a viable career option for some. Although starting pay can be painfully low, captains at the larger regional Airlines will see their salaries grow to between $60,000 and $100,000 depending on the airline and type of aircraft flown. The current minimum experience requirements for regional airlines are quite low. They tend to range anywhere from 700 hours total time with 50 hours of multi-engine time to 1500 hours of total time and 200 hours of multi-engine time. Keep in mind that these are "minimums" and the average pilot hired is likely to have somewhat more experience. However, there is no reason not to apply as soon as you meet the requirements. Recent changes in FAA regulations will require all pilots hired by the airlines to have an ATP certificate or the new "restricted ATP." The "restricted ATP" will be available with 750 hours for military trained pilots, at 1,000 hours for graduates of approved four year college aviation programs, and 1,250 hours for graduates of approved two year associates degree programs.

A proven way to improve your chances of being hired by regional is to gain experience flying in a Part 135 air charter environment as well as building some flight time in turbine powered aircraft.

Which regional(s) should you apply to? That depends on your goals. There are number of things to keep in mind.

- What type of aircraft do they fly? Turboprops? Jets? Both?
- Where will I be based? Am I willing to move there? Will it be practical to commute?
- How quickly can I upgrade to captain? If your goal is to land a job at a major airline this is a critical question. Many of the majors require or prefer 1000 of pilot in command time at a Part 135 or 121 air carrier. Obviously the sooner you can upgrade the sooner you can log your 1000 hours. You don't want to become trapped as a high time first officer with little or no PIC time.
- Is there a "flow-through" agreement? Some regional airlines have flow-through agreements with their major

airline affiliate or parent companies to give preferential hiring treatment to the pilots flying for that regional.

- Pay. Don't become *overly* fixated on pay. There are multiple factors that go into near term job satisfaction and the long term career benefit of a particular job. First year pay at virtually every regional airline stinks! However, if you are considering a job at a regional airline as a career, then pay, benefits, retirement, etc. are much more important than for the pilot looking to build experience and move on as quickly as possible.

- Training contracts. Most companies don't have these but a few do. As a condition of employment they will ask you to sign a training contract. Basically they're asking you to agree to reimburse them $10,000 or $15,000 if you leave the company in less than a year. The terms vary, but you get the idea. On one hand, you can understand why a company would ask for a minimum commitment in return for spending a significant amount of money on your training. On the other hand, this could be a warning sign that the company is not a great place to work and can't keep employees. Don't dismiss a company that requires a training contract outright. But do check them out a little closer than those who don't.

## Major Airlines

For many pilots, flying for a major airline is their ultimate goal or "dream job". It is not hard to understand why. The job and the lifestyle is basically the same as that of a regional airline pilot. But you will be flying larger aircraft, have better schedules and higher pay. The average captain for a major airline works 14 days per month and earns around $150,000 per year. In addition to the pay, there are other draws to flying for the majors as well. You will have the opportunity to fly the "heavy iron". You may have the opportunity to fly international routes for some airlines. And there is a certain amount of prestige associated with being a pilot for a major airline that is important to some.

After a difficult decade that included a number of bankruptcies, downsizings and mergers, the major airlines are projected to see significant growth going forward. The good news for pilots coming up through the ranks today is that professional pilots *will* be in demand by airlines large and small. The time for you to prepare, build experience and get qualified for these jobs is now.

So, what is the best route to a job at a major airline? All of the advice and actions required to land a job at a regional airline apply to obtaining a position at one of the majors. Specific experience and qualifications that will improve your odds of being hired include:

- PIC time in turbine powered aircraft. Some majors require 1000 hours PIC in a turboprop or jet. Often, a higher value is placed on flight time logged in a Part 121 (airline) environment. This is why pilots wanting to land a job at a major airline should look to upgrade to the captain's seat as quickly as possible (if flying for a regional airline or charter operator). No matter how much total time a first officer at a regional airline has, he will find it difficult to make the leap to a major until he is able to log a sufficient amount of PIC time.
- A college degree. If you have not completed a four degree program you want to consider doing so. Not every major airline requires a degree but virtually all "prefer" it. There are many opportunities to complete your degree both part-time and online. You will find a directory of college programs in chapter 16.

- Recommendations. Recommendations can be "helpful" in obtaining a job at a regional airline but is *critical* at certain major airlines. Start growing your network and building those relationships now!
- Type Ratings. Having a type rating in the type of aircraft airline flies is often helpful. Southwest Airlines is famous for requiring pilots to obtain a 737 type rating prior to being hired. Fortunately this is not the case with most airlines. In general, I don't recommend obtaining a type rating unless you *know* you to be able to use it. At a cost of around $10,000+ that may be money better invested elsewhere.

## Air Charter

There are many thousands of pilots flying for air charter operators. Air charter companies operate under "Part 135" of the FAA regulations. These operations range in size from a single pilot flying a single-engine aircraft to multi-plane, multi-pilot operations utilizing transport category aircraft. The basic requirements for pilots are:

VFR = Commercial pilot with Instrument rating. 500 hours total time, 100 hours cross-country, 25 hours cross-country at night.

IFR = commercial pilot with instrument rating. 1200 hrs. total time, 500 hours cross-country, 100 hours night, 75 hours instrument time (50 of which are in an aircraft)

Pilots can earn well over $100,000 per year when flying heavier jets such as a Gulfstream or Challenger. Captains of turboprops such as the King Air can expect to earn the $50-$70,000 per year range. Many pilots enjoy the variety that comes with flying charter. The link below is a searchable database you can use to locate charter operators by location.

**http://av-info.faa.gov/OpCert.asp?SrchBy=Location**

## Corporate Aviation

Corporate pilots fly a variety of aircraft owned by corporations to transport executives and other personnel to branch locations, meetings, conferences etc. Some corporate flight departments may be as small as a single light twin. Others may include a fleet of jets. A corporate flying job is difficult to describe because of the significant variations from company to company and types of aircraft flown. But in general a corporate pilot can expect significantly more variety with regard to his destinations in work schedule than an airline pilot might. While pilots at larger flight departments may have a fixed schedule, pilots at smaller flight departments are often "on call". A corporate pilot, particularly when flying jet aircraft will frequently be compensated far better than a regional airline pilot. This is particularly true for the first few years at a regional airline. The pilots of heavier aircraft such as a Gulfstream frequently earn *well over* $100,000 annually and can often match or exceed the pay received by major airline pilots. One of the major benefits of corporate aviation versus the airlines is the ability to make a lateral move from one company to another and to "leapfrog" into considerably better jobs and larger equipment. When an airline pilot moves from one company to another he must start at the bottom of the list again and work his way up based on seniority. A corporate pilot who does a good job of cultivating his network can often land his "dream job" years ahead of an airline pilot. An interesting career option for many is to fly for a "fractional" jet ownership company such as Netjets or Flexjet. This is somewhat of a hybrid between corporate and airline flying. You will be flying corporate type aircraft, but have a fixed schedule and typically be ranked within a "seniority" system similar to that of an airline.

## Civil Service

Both the federal government and state governments operate numerous aircraft. Governments operate everything from Piper Super Cubs to helicopters and from King Airs to large jets. In addition to the opportunity to do some interesting flying these jobs typically offer competitive pay and above-average job security. Currently, 16 federal departments and agencies own operate approximately 1485 aircraft with a billion-dollar annual budget. This is in addition to the many aircraft operated by state governments and law enforcement agencies.

## Cargo Airlines

There are many dedicated cargo carriers. The premier companies such as FedEx and UPS offer excellent pay and benefits that exceed that of most major airlines. This type of flying offers a different experience than flying passengers does. But as one of my cargo flying friends put it, "boxes don't complain". Flying for some of the smaller cargo operations is an excellent way to build high-quality flight time. Although there are jobs flying multi-engine piston aircraft there is also a large fleet of turboprops aircraft such as the Cessna Caravan, Beech 99, Beach 1900, etc. In addition, companies like Amerijet and Airnet have fleets that include Lear Jets, Falcon Jets and DC-9's. International air cargo companies such as Polar Air Cargo, Kalitta and others fly aircraft as large as 747's.

## Aerial Application (Crop Dusting)

"Crop dusting" or aerial application as it is now referred to, is far different than most people imagine. These are not pilots out "hot dogging" over farm fields. It is a highly specialized kind of flying requiring a great deal of precision. Most states require pilots to obtain a state specific "aerial applicator's license". For thousands of pilots it has proven to be a very rewarding career choice. Ag Pilots, as they refer to themselves, are often flying sophisticated turbine powered aircraft, have the potential to earn a six-figure income and may have several months off each year. Pilots frequently start off as part of the ground crew loading aircraft and learning about the different types of pesticides, fertilizers, etc. Some operators may be willing to train you on the job assuming you already have good basic flying skills and a good work ethic. In addition, there are several schools that train aspiring ag pilots such as Ag-Flight in Georgia and Flying Tigers in Louisiana. Today the average Ag Pilot is over 50 years old. There is and will continue to be a demand for hard working young pilots to enter the field. If you have an interest I would suggest contacting the National Agricultural Aviation Association. They can provide you with a great deal of information about this industry. www.agaviation.org

**Aerial Firefighting**
A wide variety of aircraft are used to help combat wildfires. These aircraft are frequently referred to as "air tankers" or "water bombers". The types of aircraft range from helicopters to single-engine agricultural type aircraft, and are often as large as four engine piston and converted heavy jet aircraft. Each fire season, the U.S. Forest Service and Bureau of Land Management operate or lease approximately 1000 aircraft. These aircraft and their pilots are instrumental in combating major forest and wildfires. There are opportunities to be a "lead" or an air tanker pilot. Lead plane pilots direct the flights of the air tankers on their respective drop runs. A variety of lead aircraft are used including the Beechcraft King Air, OV-10 Bronco, Cessna 0-2 Skymaster and others. Air tanker pilots fly the aircraft on runs dropping either water or fire retardant chemicals. This type of flying is seasonal and as you might

imagine more hazardous than most. Many of the pilots are current or former ag pilots who benefit from their experience in similar aircraft types and with low altitude operations.

## Bush Flying
For pilots seeking a bit more adventure, bush flying may fit the bill. There are many opportunities for pilots in both Alaska and northern Canada. Often, relatively low time pilots are able to get jobs in Alaska flying Cessna 206's and similar aircraft. Having a seaplane rating and experience with float equipped aircraft will open up additional opportunities. There are also numerous jobs in remote areas around the world flying for relief agencies, the United Nations and charitable organizations.

## Flying Abroad
Aviation is growing rapidly in many parts of the world. Currently Asia is seeing some of the most rapid growth. Airlines in many countries hire foreign pilots to fly for their airlines. It is not unusual to see contract jobs paying between $10,000 and $20,000 per month plus housing and benefits. Corporate flying jobs in Asia and the Middle East can also pay exceptionally well. In addition to the high pay and benefits, pilots get a potential added bonus of having most of their salary free from federal income tax.

## The Military Option
The Armed Forces may be a viable option for some aspiring pilots. All branches of the military have pilot positions. If you qualify and are accepted into a pilot training program you will receive some of the very best training in the world. In exchange, you will be required to commit to a minimum number of years in active duty service. And it goes without

saying that your service may include defending our country overseas if asked. To learn more about aviation opportunities with the US armed forces contact a local recruiter and seek out friends or family members who may be serving in the military branch you are interested in. Below are links to the various military websites.

| U.S. Army | U.S. Navy |
|---|---|
| www.goarmy.com | www.navy.com |
| **U.S. Air Force** | **Air Force National Guard** |
| www.af.mil | www.afreserve.com |
| **U.S. Marine Corps** | **U.S. Coast Guard** |
| www.marines.com | www.uscg.mil |

# CHAPTER 9

## TIME BUILDING

### Time Building

Many low time pilots feel caught in the Catch-22 of needing more flight time in order to get a flying job and needing to land a flying job in order to build more flight time. Here are a few ideas for building experience on a budget.

### Safety Pilot

When a pilot wants to practice flying instrument approaches, particularly "under the hood", he is required to be accompanied by a qualified safety pilot. The primary job of the safety pilot is to watch for traffic and be the "eyes" for the pilot who is flying strictly with reference to his flight instruments. Because the safety pilot is a required crewmember both pilots can legally log pilot in command time. If you're flight school or FBO has a bulletin board, why not post a note saying "Safety Pilot Available"? You can do another pilot a favor and build valuable flight time at no cost.

### Share Costs

While you can't legally "charge" your friends, family or others to fly them places in a rented Cessna 172, it is legal to "share" the cost proportionately. If you have friends that are willing to share the cost of a two-hour flight to the beach you may have the opportunity to build flight time at a 50% to 75% reduction in cost.

## Sweat Equity
Sometimes flight schools or FBO's are willing to trade flight time for labor such as washing aircraft. You may also have other skills to barter with. Are you a good bookkeeper? Do you know how to build a website? Think about it. You may have a skill set to barter with that's more valuable than you might imagine.

## Ferry Aircraft
Aircraft dealers often need the assistance of "ferry pilots" to pick up and deliver aircraft around the country. This could be a great way to build cross-country time. Introduce yourself to as many aircraft dealers as possible and let them know you're available.

## Aerial Photography
If you have talent as a photographer (or know someone who does) you may be able to both build flight time and earn an income offering aerial photography services. Real estate brokers and developers often need this service. You might consider contacting local photographers to strike up a partnership if this type of work appeals to you.

## Block Time
If you have the money available, it can make sense to purchase "block time". Many flight schools and FBO's will give you a discount for buying aircraft rental in blocks of 10, 50 or even more hours. There are a number of companies that specialize in offering multi-engine block time in 50 and 100 hour increments. For example, pilots will often have built the total flight time needed to qualify for a regional airline position but lack the 50, 100 or 200 hours of multiengine time required. Purchasing block time may be a viable solution. I was in the position myself of having a sufficient amount of total time but

was a bit short on multiengine time. I bought a 50 hour block of multi-engine time and in just a couple of weeks time I was able to meet the minimums for the job I was seeking. As an added bonus a flight instructor friend split the cost of several of those hours with me. He built some valuable multiengine time while helping me to sharpen my instrument skills. You may also come across companies which allow you to build flight time as a first officer with a part 135 or 121 air carrier. Depending upon your budget you may be flying anything from a piston engine twin to a heavy jet. These programs are typically expensive (in the total cost, not per hour) but do provide valuable training and experience. Some have criticized these programs for "stealing jobs" or forcing pilots to "buy their job". You'll have to determine for yourself if these programs would be of benefit to you.

## Civil Air Patrol

What if you could build flight time affordably while doing some good at the same time? If this interests you, the CAP may present an opportunity for you. CAP owns the largest fleet of single-engine piston aircraft in the nation, primarily Cessna 172s and 182s, and CAP pilots fly those planes to perform CAP missions in service to their local communities. CAP pilots fly reconnaissance missions for homeland security, search and rescue, disaster relief, and even counterdrug operations at the request of government or law enforcement agencies. They sometimes transport medical personnel and supplies and blood and live tissue. In times of disaster, they assess damage and transport emergency personnel from site to site. When not flying traditional emergency missions, cadet orientation pilots will have the opportunity to fly orientation rides for cadets and teachers. The Civil Air Patrol's aircraft are located at strategic locations throughout the nation to be readily available when missions arise. CAP members maintain these aircraft at the highest levels of safety and efficiency and have access to specialists at CAP National headquarters for maintenance, safety and training questions.

If you do become CAP pilot, you will perform some of the organizations most important work. CAP is also a great place for you to meet and work with people who share your interest in flying and want to use their skills in a meaningful way. You can find more information at www.gocivilairpatrol.com.

## Should You Buy an Airplane?

You may be wondering about the wisdom of purchasing an airplane in order to save money in your effort to build flight time. The safe thing to do is recommend that you stick to renting and purchasing block time. *However,* if you have the financial wherewithal to purchase an airplane it is in fact *possible* to come out ahead financially. I have owned several single-engine airplanes and have always managed to resell them for at least what I paid. With some hunting you can locate an older Cessna 150 with a mid-time engine for under $20,000. Older Cessna 172 can be had routinely for under $40,000. If you have done your homework and paid the right price for the aircraft your risk is really one of maintenance. You don't want an aircraft in need of a significant amount of deferred maintenance which you will end up paying for. Beware of the "fixer upper". The idea is to purchase an airplane which you can fly for several hundred hours at a cost below that of renting and still be able to sell the aircraft for at least what you paid to acquire it. Keep in mind that this is a gamble. A major unscheduled maintenance event can quickly consume any savings. Below is an analysis using hypothetical costs for a light single engine airplane.

### Sample Cost Analysis

| Fixed Costs | Annual |
|---|---|
| Hangar / Tie Down | $1000 |
| Insurance | $1200 |
| Payment | $0 |
| **Variable Costs** | **Hourly** |
| Fuel / Oil | $50 |
| Maintenance | $10 |
| Overhaul Reserves | $8 |

| Cost Per Hour Based on the Costs Above | 100 Hours Per Year | 300 Hours Per Year | 500 Hours Per Year |
|---|---|---|---|
| | $90 Hour | $75 Hour | $72.50 Hour |

If you do decide to purchase an aircraft for the purpose of building time and experience, keep the following thoughts in mind.

- Stick to the low end of the price range. You can lose a lot more money buying a $130,000 airplane than you can buy a $30,000 airplane.
- Purchase an aircraft that is IFR equipped and certified. You want to be able to do your instrument training and/or sharpen your instrument skills in your airplane.

- Avoid complex and multi-engine aircraft. Unless you have very deep pockets stick with single-engine fixed gear aircraft. The risk of large maintenance bills is simply too great, *especially* with twins.
- Consider a partner. Having a partner will lower your annual "fixed" costs by 50%.
- Consider a "lease back". Sometimes, flight schools will allow you to place your aircraft on "leaseback" with them. This is an arrangement where the flight school will lease the aircraft out in its rental pool. As the owner, you share in the revenue generated. While this can defray some of your ownership costs I would not recommend this if your primary goal is to build flight time. In a leaseback arrangement you will lose the scheduling flexibility that owning your own aircraft affords.
- Seek advice from a knowledgeable mechanic or maintenance shop. You will want to have a thorough "pre-buy inspection" conducted on any aircraft prior to purchase. They can also assist you in estimating ongoing maintenance costs.

# CHAPTER 10

# THE JOB HUNT

## The Job Hunt

### Networking

Networking is one of the vital keys to your success as a professional pilot. Some pilots are reluctant to network effectively because they fear being seen as being self-serving, pushy or overly aggressive. Don't make the mistake of thinking that networking is about "using" other people. What networking is really about is building relationships. For pilot seeking a job with an airline, people in your network can give you a heads up on who may be hiring and when. They can provide you with letters of recommendation and even personally walk your resume into the chief pilots' office. For pilots seeking a career as a corporate pilot networking is even more critical. As often as not, corporate flying jobs are never even advertised. They are filled by word-of-mouth and with the recommendation of existing crewmembers. Effective networking can lead you to a job opportunity *before* it is announced or even available. If you simply wait around for jobs to be advertised you will place yourself in competition with any number of other qualified candidates. But having someone in your network recommend you for an upcoming position can put you on the short list to be interviewed and potentially hired. People prefer to work with people that they know and like. If you are already known by a potential employer or one of his key employees you will have a significant advantage.

## Networking Tips

**Make a written list**. You should have a written list of people you *already* know who may be helpful in leading you to a job. Chances are you already have a lot more people in your network then you realize. It is important to maintain a physical written list of your contacts. You don't want to be digging through a drawer hoping to find that business card the chief pilot from XYZ gave you last year. As you make new contacts, add them to your list or file. After your skills and qualifications, your network is your most valuable asset. It is worth the effort to be particularly well organized and strategic in this area.

**Reach out to your network**. Let your key contacts know what kind of job you're looking for and what your current situation is. Remember, you only have one set of eyes and ears. Reaching out to your network will multiply your chances of learning about excellent opportunities.

**Keep your network informed**. If you land a job, or your situation changes let them know. Don't waste the time of an important contact by not keeping them updated. If you do, they're not likely to keep you high on their list to help in the future.

**Be thoughtful.** If your contact is especially busy, be respectful of their time. As you reconnect with former classmates and coworkers make sure you are friendly and offer to help them as well. Always be sure and follow-up with anyone who helps you by providing a good lead or referral. Not every referral will result in a job, but you *must* follow-up and be appreciative for their assistance. If you simply disappear and turn up again six months later asking for help again, you're not likely to get it.

**Cultivate Your Network.** You don't want to be "that guy" who only calls or makes contact when he needs something. Any good relationship is a two-way street. Don't make every contact simply about helping yourself. If your contact is a friend, then don't forget to *be a friend*. When it comes to professional contacts, be cognizant of what you can do for them. If you have the opportunity to refer them business, forward an article that may be helpful, etc. invest the time to do it. There is a rule in business that applies here as well. *Give value first.*

**Be Specific.** As you reach out to specific individuals in your network think about what it is you're looking for. Can they refer you to a job or potential employer? Do you need a reference from them? Can they provide you with an introduction to someone you would like to meet?

**Don't ask for a job.** Asking directly for a job puts your contact under the gun and in the uncomfortable situation of having to turn you down. The *smart* thing to do is ask for "advice". The worst thing that could happen is that you get some advice that may well be helpful and useful in your job hunt. Obviously there is the possibility that they would be able to hire you now or in the future, or know someone who can.

**How to add "*Golden Contacts*" to your network.**

With a little bit of effort, there is *no one* you can't reach. I was able to meet the chief pilots from two Fortune 500 flight departments by simply picking up the phone and calling them. At the time I was flying for an airline and was considering making the move to corporate flying. The problem was that I didn't know anyone flying corporate in the city I was going to move to. What do you do? Do your research and pick up the phone! Now at this point I was not trying to land a job. Rather, I was growing my network for the future. When I contacted these gentlemen by phone I introduced myself and told them that I was looking to transition to corporate flying "a year or two in the future". I explained that I was not looking for a job at this time, but rather was hoping they might be willing to meet with me and give me a few minutes of their time to share their advice and insights with regard to a career as a corporate pilot. This resulted in two very helpful meetings and several excellent contacts. Why did they give me their time? It was simply because I was a fellow pilot who asked for their help and advice. I did not ask for a job or for anything other than to share a bit of their experience and advice with me. Do not go into a meeting like this and hand them your resume! They will ask you for your resume should they want it. I would encourage you to keep at least "one step ahead" using this method. By that I mean making contacts that can help you with your *next* career step. There is nothing wrong with going door to door looking for flying job. Just be honest about it. If you are going to talk to them about hiring you now then say so in advance. Arranging a meeting under false pretenses would do far more harm than good. You will find that "airplane people" are some of the best in the world. It's hard to imagine an industry where people are more passionate about what they do and are more willing to help one another succeed. There's a tremendous amount of valuable advice you can get by simply asking for it. I would encourage you to stay ahead of the game. Don't just focus on contacts that can help you today. Cultivate relationships with people that can help you one, three or five years down the road.

## Keeping Track of Your Search
It is critical that your job search is documented and well organized. You should have a record of *every* resume you send, online application you submit and contact you make. You can use an Excel spreadsheet, a three ring binder or any other system that works for you. The key point here is that you must have a system and that you *use it* without fail. It would be wise to incorporate a calendar into your system so that you can send updated resumes at the appropriate intervals.

## Internet Resources
There are numerous websites related to pilot jobs. A quick search on Google will give you dozens of results. Some reputable paid sites include www.planejobs.com and www.findapilot.com, but there are many more. There are also numerous free sites and forums. While the forums can be interesting and sometimes informative, take the advice and information offered with a grain of salt. It is often third party information posted by anonymous inexperienced "wanna be" pilots. Use your judgment and make sure any advice you plan to implement comes from someone who has "been there and done that".

## Your Online Reputation
It is *very* common for employers to search online for information about job candidates. *Don't* make assumptions

about what an employer can or cannot see about you on social media websites. Do not post any inappropriate or controversial pictures, comments, jokes, etc. and delete any that may already exist asap. There is little point in putting great effort into looking professional on paper if your online persona is that of an immature party animal.

# Recruiters
## Pilot Recruitment/Pilot Leasing Companies
There are number of pilot recruitment and pilot leasing companies. These companies provide the service of locating and providing pilots to work as contractors or full time employees for other firms. Some of these firms provide selection and screening services for companies seeking pilots.

**AeroProfessional**
**www.aeroprofessional.com**

**Aviationcv.com**
**www.aviationcv.com**

**Betts Recruitment Limited**
**www.bettsrecruitment.com**

**Confair Recruitment**
**www.confairrecruitment.com**

**Contractair**
**www.contractair.net**

**Crew Resources Worldwide**
**www.crewresourcesworldwide.com**

**Direct Personnel**
www.directpersonnel.com

**Flight Crew International**
www.flightcrewint.com

**Hawaii Aviation**
www.hawaiiaviation.com

**GAP Aviation**
www.gapaviation.com

**IAC Global**
www.iacglobal.com/

**IASCO**
www.iasco.com

**Next Generation Aviation Recruiters**
www.nexgen-aviation.com

**Paramount Aviation Resources Group**
www.paramountarg.com

**Parc Aviation**
www.parcaviation.aero

**PAS Aviation Group**
www.pas-aviation.aero

**Protec Technical**
www.protectechnical.co.uk/employers/#aircrew

**Rishworth Aviation**
www.rishworthaviation.com

**Sigma Aviation Services**
www.sigmaraviation.com

**Storm Aviation**
www.stormaviation.com

**Soft Touch Aviation**
www.softtouchaviation.com

**Total Aviation Service**
www.flytas.com

**WASINC**
www.wasinc.net/en

**World Airline Services**
www.world-airline-services.com

**Zenon Aviation Recruitment**
www.zenon.aero

**Airline Directory**
www.airlineupdate.com

## Airline Flying Jobs

Airline flying jobs are relatively easy to research. The airline's website will often tell you whether they are currently hiring, outline the minimum qualifications and tell you how to apply. This is where a well cultivated network can really pay off, particularly at the major airlines. Assuming you are otherwise qualified, a reference or referral from a current employee can be the difference between landing an interview or being just another resume in the pile. Your goal should be to have your resume personally handed to the chief pilot or HR person by a pilot currently employed at the airline. There is no better way than this to get your resume to the top of the stack. In addition, one or more letters of recommendation from current pilots can be a big help in getting you an interview.

Each airline has a preferred method for pilots to apply. Some want you to fax or e-mail a resume. Others have an online application process. Pay close attention to the instructions and recommendations and follow them perfectly. If the instructions say "resume by e-mail preferred" don't send it by fax. Remember, you are being evaluated from your very first contact. Be sure and keep copies of any applications and documents you submit to a potential employer. You may be filling out the same or similar forms in the future and it is important that the information you provide is consistent.

If the airline recommends that you update your application "every six months", do so in a timely manner. If the airline does not specify how often to update your information, three months is a good interval. The exception would be a significant update such as completing a degree program or earning a 737 type rating, etc.

## Corporate Flying Jobs

A successful career in corporate aviation requires top-notch networking skills. Unlike an airline job which is seniority-based, corporate pilots have the potential to "leap frog" other pilots and land a "dream job" relatively fast. Locating the flight departments for major corporations is relatively easy. Smaller operations can be more difficult to identify. Here are some thoughts on finding opportunities others may miss.

- Many major airports have a list of the airport's tenants on their website. You will often find corporate flight departments listed here.
- Aircraft maintenance shops typically know what corporate aircraft are on the field and who owns them.
- Aircraft brokers are also familiar with corporate aircraft and flight departments in the area.
- Let's say for example that you are looking for a job in Dallas Texas and have experience flying Beechcraft King Airs. In addition to all of the traditional strategies, here is a clever tactic that few pilots utilize. The FAA keeps registration information on every aircraft in the United States and has a searchable database! A quick online search of Dallas County Texas will show the names and addresses of more than 20 King Air owners. Corporate flight departments are often low key and not highly visible. This is a great resource to locate hidden opportunities in corporate aviation.
- You can conduct your own search at:

http://registry.faa.gov/AircraftInquiry/statecounty_inquiry.aspx

**References and Letters of Recommendation**

You want your references and letters of recommendation to carry the most weight possible, so they need to come from the right source.

**Current Employees.** A letter of recommendation from a pilot currently flying the line at the airline or flight department you're applying with can be very helpful. The employer is going to know that this pilot is putting his own reputation on the line in recommending you. They would also assume that a current employee would never recommend hiring a pilot who they felt was unsafe or difficult work with. Ideally the letter should come from a pilot has been employed long enough to have completed their probationary period. A letter from a pilot hired last month will not carry the same weight.

**Employers.** Previous employers have had the chance to evaluate your piloting skills, work ethic, professionalism and ability to work well with other employees. A letter from your chief pilot or direct supervisor is best. Letters from coworkers are acceptable but are not as strong. If you receive a letter of recommendation which is poorly written, or uses such soft and conditional language that it amounts to a luke warm recommendation, don't use it.

# CHAPTER 11

## YOUR RESUME

**Resumes**

Virtually all potential employers are going to expect you to provide a resume when applying for a position. It is absolutely *critical* that your resume is as professional and impressive as possible. Unlike an application form supplied by an employer, the resume is your first opportunity to demonstrate your level of professionalism and high standards. This is your opportunity to highlight the skills and qualifications that your potential employer will find most appealing. Frequently, your resume will be right in front of the person interviewing you. Be sure that you're prepared to answer questions about everything in your resume. While a sharp looking resume does not guarantee you'll get a job or even an interview, one which is poorly laid out or contains spelling mistakes may well go straight into the trash can. Your resume is a key to helping you make that all-important "good first impression". Here are some key points with regard to resumes.

- **The paper.** Your resume should be printed *only* on high-quality bond or linen paper. The paper should be white or off-white in color. Don't make the mistake of trying to stand out from the crowd by printing your resume on brightly colored paper. So what is wrong with printing your resume in a piece of plain white copy paper? There's nothing "wrong" with it. It simply does not look as good or make the same impression that high-quality paper does. I actually had a friend tell me that he did not want to "waste" the money on the "expensive" paper. We are literally talking about a nickel or dime per resume. Do you really want to surrender even the slightest edge in your job hunt over a nickel? Think about it from the perspective of the employer. Two similarly qualified pilots send you their resumes, but you don't currently have a position open. Which resume are you going to save for future reference? The poorly formatted one on cheap paper or the professional looking one? Have you ever kept a piece of "junk" mail or other publication around that you didn't need only because it seemed "too nice" to throw away? Use human nature to your advantage. If someone tosses my resume in the trash I want them to at least feel guilty about it!

- **Electronic Format.** Some employers may request that you submit your resume via e-mail. Your resume should be created in Microsoft Word or converted to a PDF file to preserve the formatting. Also, be sure and name your resume file appropriately. Don't simply name it "resume". The potential employer will likely have many resumes on file and you want him to be able to identify yours. An example would be "John Smith Resume.doc".

- **The font.** Choose a font that is easy to read. Avoid script or other overly "ornate" fonts. If in doubt use Times Roman, Arial or a substantially similar font. Do not use multiple fonts, but rather a single font throughout your resume. You can use bold type, underline and adjust the font size as needed.

- **Length.** If at all possible limit your resume to a single page. Your objective is to highlight your qualifications and credentials in a professional and concise manner.

When a potential employer looks at your resume, you want them to know in a matter of seconds that you're qualified for the job. While it is important that you highlight all relevant experience, avoid overly verbose or obviously "overinflated" descriptions of your previous positions.

- **Heading.** The heading should include your name (in bold print), your full mailing address, your phone number and e-mail address. Putting the word "resume" at the top of the page is not necessary. If you're having any difficulty condensing your resume to one page leave it off.

- **Phone number.** Use a phone number where you can be easily reached. Taking too long to return a call can mean missing an interview opportunity. A cell phone number is fine as long as a caller can leave a message. Make sure that your outgoing message is professional. This is not the place to exhibit your love of rap music. A simple message which *includes your name* stating that you will promptly return the call is sufficient.

- **Mailing address.** Use the physical address where you are living if possible. Knowing your location will assist the potential employer in coordinating an interview and know if there will be a need to ask you to move your residence.

- **E-mail address.** Use an e-mail address that is simple and professional. Using an e-mail address like studpilot@yahoo.com is not a good idea. If you have an e-mail address that you're using specifically for your job hunt, make sure that you are checking it regularly.

- **Objective** or **Position Sought**. In most cases this should simply read "Flight Crew Member" or "First Officer Position" if you are applying to an airline. The exception would be when you're responding to an ad for a specific position such as "Lear 60 Captain". Avoid using language such as "a rewarding career in which I can utilize my talents to blah, blah, blah". Your resume is not the place for this. You can relate this sort of information in your cover letter and during your interview.

- **Qualifications**. This is the area in which you list your flight time and ratings. Include your ratings such as "Commercial Pilot, Multi-Engine Land, Instrument". Include FCC Radiotelephone Operator Permit: Restricted (assuming you hold one), and information on your medical such as "FAA First Class Medical Certificate: 11/2014". Pilots with experience in heavy or jet aircraft will want to use the following categories for flight experience: Total Time, Multi-Engine, Turbojet, Turbine, Pilot in Command, Second in Command Turbojet. An additional category would be your time in an aircraft relevant to the position you're applying for. If you are applying for a job flying a Citation X and have 700 hours in type you want list that specifically. For lower time pilots with primarily piston engine aircraft experience the following categories are appropriate: Total Time, Pilot in Command, Multi-Engine, Multi-Engine PIC, Cross Country, Night. It is neither necessary nor productive to break your time down any further. Low time pilots will sometimes add categories or breakdowns to create the illusion of additional experience. This practice will only make your resume less appealing and more difficult to assess quickly.

- **Types of Aircraft Flown**. I would suggest leaving this out. You'll be listing the types of aircraft you have flown in your work history and it is not necessary to list them again. If you sat right seat in a King Air for one hour do you really want to list it? An interviewer could easily see that and ask you technical questions about the aircraft you would not be able to answer.

- **Work Experience**. In this section you will want to list the name and address of each employer, the dates you were employed, and a brief description of your job such as "Captain C421, FAR Part 135, passenger and cargo charter operations throughout the Midwest". If at all possible avoid leaving any significant gaps in employment. Conversely it is not necessary to list the part-time job at a fast food restaurant you held to supplement your income. The actual job application is the place for this sort of information. That said, you want your resume to be both truthful and accurate. Remember that lying on your resume could not only prevent you from getting the job in the first place but could easily get you fired from the job if a serious deception is discovered at a later date.

- **Education and Training**. In this section you will list your formal education. If you have a college degree it is not necessary to list your High School. List the school, dates you attended, your major and the degree you achieved. If you did not complete your degree, simply list your major and the dates you attended. If you had a GPA of 3.0 or higher, list that as well.

- **Interests**. It is not necessary to include this section. However, this could be a place to include certain skills that an employer may find beneficial. For example if you are a volunteer EMT with first aid and medical training or possess language skills, those would be positives.

- **References**. I would recommend *not* putting the typical "references available upon request" line at the bottom of your resume. Is there any reason for employer to think they would "not" be available upon request? And if you do possess glowing letters of recommendation why not simply include them?

## Cover Letters

In addition to the traditional formalities, your cover letter is your opportunity to express what makes you a great candidate in *addition* to the qualifications listed on your resume. It should be printed on the same high quality paper as your resume. Below are some examples of things you should consider including in your cover letter.

- ✓ A strong team player / work well with others.
- ✓ A willingness to relocate.
- ✓ Specific experience relevant to the job (time in the same aircraft type, type rating, etc.)
- ✓ A willingness to obtain additional training.
- ✓ Additional training / ratings / education in progress.

In general terms your resume is to sell your qualifications and your cover letter is to sell <u>you</u>. You want to convey the reasons you would make an excellent employee and coworker. Don't underestimate the power of a well crafted cover letter.

# (Sample Resume)
## John Q. Smith

12345 Main St.
Mytown, CA 30001
Phone: 555.555.5555
E-mail: johnsmith@gmail.com

---

**OBJECTIVE**

**Flight Crew Position**

**QUALIFICATIONS**

- Airline Transport Pilot: Airplane Multi Engine Land Instrument
- Dornier D-328JET Type Rating
- Flight Instructor: Airplane Single Engine Land
- FAA Ground Instructor: Advanced
- FAA First Class Medical Certificate:
- FCC Radiotelephone Operator Permit

**FLIGHT TIME**

**2,453 Total Hours**

| | |
|---|---|
| 1,748 PIC | 980 CFI |
| 1,035 PIC jet | 217 Actual instruments |
| 1,170 Multiengine | 405 Night |

**EXPERIENCE**

**Captain: Dornier 328JET**
Big Time Aviation, Inc. | Los Angeles, CA
Part 135 charter operations domestic and international
-2010 to present

**Captain: Beech 99**
Wing and a Prayer Skydiving, Inc. | Dallas, TX
Jump pilot for skydiving operation.
-2009 to 2010

**Flight Instructor**
Crosswind Aviation, Inc. | Miami, FL
Primary and Advanced Part 141 instruction in Piper and Cessna aircraft
-2007 to 2009

**EDUCATION**

**BS in Business Administration**
University of Miami | Miami, FL
3.20 GPA

# (Sample Cover Letter)

### John Q. Smith
12345 Main St.
Mytown, CA 30001
Phone: 555.555.5555
E-mail: johnsmith@gmail.com

Mr. Robert Jones
Chief Pilot
Mega Airlines
100 Airplane Rd.
Chicago, IL 45987                                   Jan. 1, 2014

Dear Mr. Jones,

I am writing to express my interest in your recently announced A-300 first officer positions.

With Mega Airlines continued success, I am confident that my experience flying domestic and international Part 135 operations would be of benefit to your airline as you recruit crewmembers for your expanding fleet.

My qualifications include:

- ATP with Dornier D-328JET Type Rating
- 2,453 Total Time; 1,748 Pilot-in-command
- BS Degree in Business Administration
- International operations


In addition to my technical qualifications, I pride myself in working well with my coworkers and always pay special attention to the most important people of all -- our customers.

With Mega's ongoing expansion, I believe that my experience, professionalism, and positive attitude would be a valuable asset to your airline. I look forward to the opportunity to interview with you soon.

Sincerely,
*John Q. Smith*
John Q. Smith

enclosure: resume, letter of recommendation

# CHAPTER 12

# MASTERING THE ART OF THE INTERVIEW

## Mastering the Art of the Interview

Assuming that an impressive resume alone is going to get you a job is a big mistake. Your resume and qualifications will only serve to help you to *get an interview*. A successful interview is what will *get you a job*. Mastering the art of the interview is very important if you want to have the most successful career possible.

What are employers looking for in a pilot?

- Maturity and professionalism.
- A good attitude.
- Safety conscious.
- Potential for advancement to captain. It is true, particularly of airlines, that they don't hire first officers but rather future captains.

- Demonstrates a passion for flying. Not just looking for a "job".
- The ability to work well with other coworkers and crewmembers.
- Loyalty to your employers.
- Self-Motivation.
- A pleasant personality. You want to present yourself as a person those interviewing you would enjoy working with. If you are being interviewed by a captain the *last* thing you want them thinking is "Man, I would hate to be stuck on a four-day trip with this guy."

The interview is the chance for the employer to learn more about you as an individual and as a potential employee. Your resume and application have answered the questions about your basic qualifications and background. But the interview will reveal what you're like as a person, your temperament, communication skills, and give some indication of your future performance on the job. The interview is your opportunity to **sell yourself**. If qualifications were all that were required, interviews would not be necessary. I'm sure you've heard of pilots with sketchy qualifications landing dream jobs. You can be sure that they have excellent interviewing skills! And with preparation and practice you will as well.

## Psychological Tests

Some companies administer a written psychological profile test. These are not tests which you can easily study or prepare for in advance. The best advice is to simply answer each question honestly. Do not over think them or attempt to give the answer "you think they want to hear". This may result in inconsistencies from one question to the next. Just read the questions carefully, answer honestly, and you should have nothing to worry about.

## Simulator Evaluation

Your interview process may include an evaluation using a flight simulator. This could be a simple desktop simulator or a much more sophisticated one. You're likely to be unfamiliar with the equipment and the instructor giving you the evaluation will be taking this into account. They're generally looking for good basic instrument skills and procedures. Do your best to maintain altitudes, headings, etc. but most of all avoid busting any minimums and demonstrate a solid command of IFR rules and procedures.

## How to Dress

It is very important that you dress appropriately for your interview. So what does "appropriately" mean? For entry-level jobs you will need to use your best judgment. It probably doesn't make much sense to show up in a suit for a job hauling skydivers in a Cessna 206. If you're familiar with the particular operation a good rule of thumb would be to come slightly better dressed than the best dressed person in the room. Airline and corporate interviews are a different story. Here you *will* wear a suit.

**Your Suit.** You will want to wear a traditional cut single breasted suit. This is not the time to be "fashion forward" or hip. If your suit is starting to show its age or fits poorly invest in a new one and have it appropriately tailored if necessary. Navy blue or dark gray are safe colors. If the suit has pinstripes make sure they are subtle. Think "conservative". You want to be confused for a banker, not a mobster or used car salesman.

**Your Shirt.** Keep it simple. Wear a clean, white, *pressed*, long-sleeved shirt.

**Your Tie**. Again, think "conservative". You can't go wrong with a solid color "power red" or dark blue silk tie. Patterns and stripes are fine as long as they are subtle. The tie should reach your belt when you're standing and be the appropriate width.

**Your Shoes.** You want to wear conservative black dress shoes. Ideally they should be new or almost new and well polished.

**Accessories**. Wear an appropriate colored belt with a *small* buckle. This is not a good time to show off your "I'd rather be flying" belt buckle. Keep your jewelry to a minimum. A pilot style watch is okay, but nothing too gaudy or flashy. Your wedding ring and class ring are fine as well but that should be the extent of your jewelry.

**Grooming** . Generally, your hair should be short and cut in a traditional style. How short? If your hair is covers your ears it is probably too long. Although a neatly trimmed mustache can be acceptable a goatee or beard are not normally permitted by airlines. Be sure your fingernails are cleaned and trimmed short and bring breath mints just in case.

## Get the Gouge
It is sometimes possible to "get the gouge" or find out in advance what to expect during a specific company's interview. These are sometimes available on various websites, but look closely at when they were posted as you'll find they are often out of date. While having this information can help put you at ease, you don't want to rely on it *too* heavily. You may well have different people conducting your interview, get asked different questions and have a very different experience.

## Tact
Tact is about showing respect for others. Be very careful not to describe any person, company or group in a disparaging

manner. Tact is the difference between saying "My last employer ran into financial difficulties and was forced to file for bankruptcy." vs. "my last employer was really shady, and skipped town owing me a month's pay." This is important not just during the interview but with every contact you make with your prospective employer from the switchboard operator and secretary on up. If an airline flies you in for an interview, it is possible that the flight crew will be aware of your presence. Be courteous and professional and don't drink any alcohol on the flight.

## Humor

Demonstrating a sense of humor can be a real positive during an interview. Just be careful that the humor is "appropriate" in nature and timing. Follow the lead of those interviewing you. If they are overly serious, you may want to save the humor for another day. If the interview is a bit more relaxed, some of humor may be appropriate. Just don't overdo it. It's okay to look like a professional with a sense of humor, you just don't want to look like a "funny guy" looking for a profession.

## Logbooks and the Documents

You are often asked to bring your log books with you to your interview. Be sure to double and triple check the flight times in your logbook before the interview. If your resume or application shows a hundred hours more flight time than your logbook does your interview can end on the spot. Be sure you have signed each page. Tab check rides and other key pages so that they are easy to find. If you have a computerized logbook be sure that you bring not only the printouts but your paper logbook with any instructor or examiner check ride sign offs as well. Be sure and bring any other documents that have been requested or that you feel will be needed. It is a good idea to bring additional copies of your resume, copies of your pilot certificates and ratings, drivers license and social security card and any letters of recommendation that were not already provided. You also want documentation and explanations regarding any violations, accidents, incidents or DUI's. There's a good chance they are already aware of the issue and you want to be ready to respond. It is better to bring copies of documents you don't need than to need a document you didn't bring. Err on the safe side. Be sure the documents are well organized and you can quickly find a document when needed.

## Do's

Pre-Interview

- Prepare copies of all documents, logbooks, transcripts, etc. you'll need for your interview.
- Study your aircraft systems, regs, Airman's Information Manual, etc.
- Research your potential employer. Review their website, news articles, etc.
- Practice! Practice answering questions. Recruit a friend or family member to help you. Practice your eye contact, handshake, tone, posture etc.
- Have your suit cleaned and shoes polished.
- Confirm your travel and hotel reservations if applicable.
- Be well rested. Don't stay up all night "cramming".

## The Interview

- Arrive 15 minutes early.
- Smile.
- Demonstrate your passion for flying.
- Be thoroughly professional.
- Maintain eye contact. (80/20 rule)

- Listen carefully to each question.
- Provide key points and supporting points in your answers.
- Provide examples when answering a question.
- Show that you put safety first.
- Don't bluff if you don't know the answer to a technical question.
- Show how you can add value.
- Be confident but don't exaggerate.

## Post-Interview

- Send thank you notes or letters.
- Critique yourself. What did you do well? Where did you fall short? Use this information to improve your performance in the future.

## Don'ts

- Don't be late.
- Don't chew gum or drink even if invited to.
- Don't disparage your current or former employers.
- Don't express how much you *need* this job.
- Don't drop the names of everyone you know that works there.
- Don't look at your watch.
- Don't rush through your answers. Answer each question thoroughly.
- Don't be the hero. Stress times you solved problems as a team rather than as an individual.
- Don't take off your coat even if offered.

## Relaxation Techniques

A certain degree of nervousness is natural during an interview. If you find yourself becoming overly nervous, do your best to relax. Slowing your breathing and taking deeper breaths is often helpful. You want to breathe from your abdomen as opposed to the chest (which is more stressful breathing). Another technique is to visualize the outcome you want in advance. Top athletes often use this method to see their "win" in advance. Also, keep in mind that the people interviewing you *want* you to have a successful interview! They did not call you in to sharpen their own interviewing skills. They need and want to hire qualified competent professional pilots. Show them that that is who you are.

## Interview Questions

There are many types of questions asked by interviewers. They generally fall into two categories, HR type questions and technical questions. Some airlines will ask you to answer numerous technical questions, while others will ask almost exclusively HR type questions. Here are some examples.

## HR Type Questions

Here are some of the most typical HR type questions. Give thought to how you would answer these and similar questions. You want your answers to be original to the degree possible and to make a positive impression. Practice answering these and other questions out loud. If you have a friend you can work with, ask each other questions and critique your answers. Just because the question looks "easy to answer" does not mean that you shouldn't prepare for it. Preparation and practice will improve your interview skills dramatically. You only have so many opportunities to present yourself to potential employers. Don't let being ill-prepared cost you the job.

1. Tell me about yourself.

2. How did you get involved in flying?
3. Where do you see yourself in 5 years?
4. Do you have any speeding tickets or other issues we should know about?
5. What was your GPA in college?
6. What are your strengths?
7. What are your weaknesses?
8. If there was one thing he could change about yourself what would it be?
9. How would your coworkers describe working with you?
10. Have you ever had an emergency? Tell us about it.
11. What makes a good or bad pilot?
12. If you could not fly for a living what would you do?
13. How would you rate your piloting skills on scale from 1 to 10?
14. We have a lot of qualified candidates, why should we hire you?
15. What goals do you have?
16. Why did you apply with us?
17. Do you know the name of our CEO?
18. Have you applied to other companies?
19. Have you ever failed a check ride? Why?
20. What would you do if you smelled alcohol on the Captains breath?
21. How much do you drink?
22. Tell me about a time you had a conflict with a passenger.
23. Tell me about a time you had a conflict with another crew member.
24. What would you do if the captain insisted on descending below minimums?

## Technical Questions.

There is a virtually infinite number of technical questions you could be asked. Below are some of the most common. It is not unusual to be asked questions about an aircraft you're currently flying or have a significant amount of time in. You will want to be ready to respond to questions about performance, speeds, weights, etc. for these aircraft. Also, make sure you understand *all* of the symbology on approach plates and en-route charts. If you do not normally use Jeppesen charts, you will need to become familiar with them as these are the ones typically used by the airlines. Studying the Airman's Information Manual and ATP test prep materials will also be beneficial.

1. Here is an approach plate, please brief the approach.
2. What is the MDA on this approach?
3. At what flight level does RVSM begin?
4. What is V1? What is V2?
5. What is zero fuel weight?
6. What is a balanced field length?
7. What is the benefit of a swept wing?
8. What is the difference between indicated airspeed and true airspeed?
9. What does it mean when the control tower flashes a red and green light signal?
10. What is a freezing rain?
11. What do vortex generators do?
12. What is the maximum speed you can fly below 10,000 feet?
13. When do you need an alternate?
14. What is the maximum speed you should use while holding?
15. What causes hydroplaning?

16. What is a mountain wave?
17. What effect does an aft CG have on aircraft performance?
18. A 747 departs while you're on final approach, what should you do?
19. What are indications of windshear?
20. If you lose sight of the runway during a circling approach, how do you execute a missed approach?
21. What is calibrated airspeed?
22. What is VMU?
23. If you are at 10,000 feet AGL what will your DME read as you pass over the station?
24. What is a critical engine?

## What Questions to Ask the Interviewer.

Frequently an interview will end with "Do you have any questions or comments for us?" This is a "catch-all" question that will give you the opportunity to add any information which you forgot or did not have the opportunity to include earlier. It will also give you the opportunity to add to or clarify answers or information that you provided during the interview. You can't get credit for skills or attributes you don't communicate during the interview. Don't ask "how you did" or "when to expect an answer". (You might not like the answer)

## Ending the Interview.

At the end of the interview you want to express your sincere thanks for having been given the opportunity to interview with the company. Thank the interviewer(s) for their time. As appropriate you can communicate that you have enjoyed both the people and process and reconfirm your desire to work for "XYZ". Obviously a firm handshake and final thank you is appropriate.

**Post-Interview.**
Be sure and send a thank you note or letter to each person who interviewed you. Follow up phone calls to ask if you will be hired are not a good idea. You will generally be told during your interview what to expect in the way of timing.

# Major Airline Screening Process

### Alaska Airlines
Technical or Aptitude Test:  No
Cognitive Testing:  No
Psychological Testing:  No
Simulator Ride:  No
Panel Interview:  Yes
One on one Interview:  Yes
Physical Exam by Company:  No

### American Airlines
Technical or Aptitude Test:  Yes
Cognitive Testing:  No
Psychological Testing:  Yes
Simulator Ride:  Yes
Panel Interview:  Yes
One on one Interview:  No
Physical Exam by Company:  Yes

### Delta Airlines
Technical or Aptitude Test:  Yes
Cognitive Testing:  Yes
Psychological Testing:  Yes
Simulator Ride:  No
Panel Interview:  Yes

One on one Interview:  No
Physical Exam by Company:  Yes

### FedEx
Technical or Aptitude Test:  Yes
Cognitive Testing:  Yes
Psychological Testing:  Yes
Simulator Ride:  Yes
Panel Interview:  Yes
One on one Interview: No
Physical Exam by Company:  Yes

### JetBlue
Technical or Aptitude Test:  No
Cognitive Testing:  No
Psychological Testing:  No
Simulator Ride:  No
Panel Interview:  Yes
One on one Interview:  Yes
Physical Exam by Company:  No

### Southwest Airlines
Technical or Aptitude Test:  No
Cognitive Testing:  No
Psychological Testing:  No
Simulator Ride:  No
Panel Interview:  Yes
One on one Interview:  Yes
Physical Exam by Company:  No

### Airtran Airlines
Technical or Aptitude Test:  No
Cognitive Testing:  No

Psychological Testing:  No
Simulator Ride:  No
Panel Interview:  Yes
One on one Interview:  No
Physical Exam by Company:  No

## United Airlines

Technical or Aptitude Test:  No
Cognitive Testing:  No
Psychological Testing:  No
Simulator Ride:  No
Panel Interview:  Yes
One on one Interview:  No
Physical Exam by Company:  No

## UPS

Technical or Aptitude Test:  No
Cognitive Testing:  No
Psychological Testing:  No
Simulator Ride:  Yes
Panel Interview:  Yes
One on one Interview:  No
Physical Exam by Company:  Yes

## US Airways

Technical or Aptitude Test:  Yes
Cognitive Testing:  Yes
Psychological Testing:  Yes
Simulator Ride:  Yes
Panel Interview:  Yes
One on one Interview:  No
Physical Exam by Company:  Yes

# CHAPTER 13

## FINANCING THE DREAM

## Financing the Dream

Few aspiring pilots have the luxury of being able to simply write a $50,000 check (or more) to pay for a career pilot program at a major flight school to obtain all of their ratings. If you're currently employed and have surplus income, you could train on a part-time basis and simply "pay as you go". This would involve training on nights and weekends and extend your training period significantly. But, upon completion you will have obtained your ratings and have the benefit of being debt free. Some pilots apply this strategy to obtaining a private license and doing some initial time building. With a private license in hand you could consider student loans to finance your advanced ratings. It is possible to obtain loans for flight training, and I have included a number of potential sources. If you do borrow money, I would encourage you to borrow only what's *absolutely necessary* and not a penny more. It will take time before you start earning any significant income, and you want the smallest loan payment possible. The easiest loans to obtain are federal student loans used to pay for an eligible Associates or Bachelors degree program. There are numerous aviation degree programs (which include flight training) that could be financed using this method. Large flight schools like American Flyers and ATP have personnel dedicated to helping you obtain funding for your flight training. You will find their contact information in the flight school directory in Chapter 17. Borrowing money to fund your flight training is a serious commitment. Don't let your enthusiasm override your better judgment. Shop around, compare rates and terms, and select the loan program that best suits your needs.

# Sources of Funding

### Pilotfinance.com
www.pilotfinance.com

### Citi Student Loans
www.studentloan.com

### Charter One Student Loans
www.charterone.com/student-services

### Discover Student Loans
www.discover.com/student-loans

### Wells Fargo Student Loans
www.wellsfargo.com/jump/EFS/studentloans

### Suntrust Student Loans
www.suntrusteducation.com

### Chase Student Loans
www.chasestudentloans.com

**USBank Student Loans**
www.usbank.com/student-lending

**Sallie Mae**
www.salliemae.com

# Federal Government Sources

The U.S. Federal government offers various programs intended to assist students finance the cost of their education at a college, university, professional, technical or vocational school in the United States. There are multiple federal programs available for U.S. citizens and permanent residents who are enrolled at least half-time as students in a degree program, who are achieving satisfactory academic progress, and who are not in default on the repayment of a grant or loan. Financial aid is typically based on financial need.

In order to receive financial assistance from the federal government, you must complete the Free Application for Federal Student Aid (FAFSA). The FAFSA is used by the U.S. Department of Education to determine your Expected Family Contribution (EFC) and eligibility for certain federal programs.

### Federal Pell Grant
Federal Pell Grants are grants that do not have to be repaid. These grants are available to undergraduate students enrolled at least half-time, based on financial need. Grant amounts will range from $400 to $4,050 depending on the estimated amount of family contribution.

## Federal Perkins Loan

The Federal Perkins loan is granted to undergraduate or graduate students enrolled at least half-time, based on financial need. This is a loan which must be paid back. Students should apply early as this program has limited funding.

## Federal Supplemental Educational Opportunity Grants

FSEOG is available to undergraduate students enrolled at least half-time, based on financial need. Assistance varies. Awards can range from $100 to $4,000 per year.

## Federal College Work-Study Program (CWSP)

CWSP is available to graduate and undergraduate students enrolled at least half-time based on need. Students may work a maximum of 20 - 25 hours per week for at least minimum wage.

## Federal Supplemental Loan for Students (SLS)

SLS is available to graduate or independent undergraduate students enrolled at least half-time. Amount available: $4,000 a year for the first and second years of undergraduate study; $5,000 for the third and fourth years of study provided the student attends a full academic year. Total funds available: $23,000 for undergraduates; $73,000 for graduate/professional students (including undergraduate amounts).

## Federal Parent Loan for Undergraduate Students (PLUS)

PLUS loans are available to the parents of dependent students to allow parents to borrow money to assist children in paying for college expenses. The student must be enrolled at least half-time. Parent loans are not based on financial need. The amount borrowed each year can be up to the college cost of attendance less other financial aid. The parent can obtain the application from a local lending institution or the Financial Aid

Office of the school you are interested in attending. There is no limit on the cumulative maximum total of the loan. However, parents cannot defer payments, which start two months after the loan is fully disbursed.

**Federal Stafford Loan Program**
All Federal Direct Stafford Loans are either subsidized (the government pays the interest during your time in school) or unsubsidized (you pay all the interest, but the payments may be deferred until post graduation). Stafford Loans are available to both undergraduate and graduate students who are enrolled at least half-time and in good standing at an eligible institution based on financial need. The maximum loans available are: $2,625 for freshmen, $3,500 for sophomores, $5,500 for juniors and seniors and $8,500 for graduate or professional students, but may not exceed $23,000 for undergraduates and $65,500 for undergraduate and graduate loans combined. You may obtain an application from a local lending institution or the Financial Aid Office of the school you plan to attend.

The US Department of Education has a comprehensive guide called "The Student Guide" with detailed information about eligibility, application processes, deadlines, types of loans and aid available, etc.

# Veterans Benefits & ROTC Scholarships

### ROTC Scholarships
Hundreds of ROTC scholarships are awarded to students every year on college campuses in the United States. The scholarships are awarded based on merit – to the most outstanding students who apply. They are awarded without regard to the financial status of the family. ROTC scholarships

will vary depending upon on the branch of military. These scholarships fund school tuition, fees, books, and possibly a monthly allowance. Scholarship recipients normally participate in summer training during college and will be required to fulfill their military obligation, which may be active duty or reserve service, after their graduation.

**Military Service Academies Scholarships**
The U.S. Military Service Academies offer both men and women an opportunity to earn a Bachelor of Science degree as well as a commission as an officer in the U.S. military. The Navy, Army, Air Force, Coast Guard and Merchant Marine each have their own Academy. Attending a service Academy provides the student with one of the best and highest ranked educations available. The Military Service Academies award full scholarships to accepted students which cover tuition, room and board and a monthly stipend to cover the cost of books, supplies, and personal needs.


**VA Benefits**
Military veterans can be eligible for reimbursement of up to 60% of expenses for their flight training. This assistance does not cover books and materials. The programs is available to students enrolled in professional pilot programs (not simply private pilot students) and are attending a Part 141 approved flight school which has been approved by the VA.
To determine your eligibility for educational assistance, you should contact the Department of Veterans Affairs (DVA) Office at (800) 827-1000

# Scholarships
Scholarships are a generally overlooked source of funding. There are literally hundreds of scholarships available. Although most are relatively modest in size, it is entirely

possible that you already meet the criteria to be awarded one or more. To follow is a partial list of sources for aviation related scholarships. Research the criteria for each, and apply for those who feel you're best qualified for. You won't get one unless you ask!

### Aero Club of New England
www.acone.org

### Aircraft Owners and Pilots Association
www.aopa.org

### Amelia Earhart Memorial Scholarships and Awards
www.ninety-nines.org

### Girls with Wings of Scholarship
www.girlswithwings.com

### Leroy Homer Foundation
www.leroyhomerjr.org/scholarships

### University Aviation Association
University aviation Association administers approximately a dozen separate scholarships. www.uaa.aero

### Airline Pilots Association
Scholarships are available for children of medically disabled members or former members of the Airline pilots Association. www.alpa.org

### Bose Corporation
Available to high school seniors and college students planning to attend Embry-Riddle Aeronautical University. www.aea.net/educationalfoundation

**Soaring Society of America**
www.ssa.org

**Joshua Mitchell Scholarship Fund**
www.grfoundation.org

**Chicago Area Business Aviation Association**
www.cabaa.com

**CAE Simuflite Citation Type Rating Scholarship**
www.uaa.aero

**Lawrence Ginocchio Aviation Scholarship**
www.nbaa.org/prodev/scholarships/ginocchio

**Regional Airline Association Scholarship**
www.raa.org/RAAHome/RAAScholarship

**Aerospace Education Foundation**
www.aef.org

**American Association of Airport Executives**
www.airportnet.org

**Aviation Distributors and Manufacturers Association**
www.adma.og

**Experimental Aircraft Association**
www.eaa.org

**Women in Aviation International**
www.wai.org

# CHAPTER 14

## SPECIFIC RATING REQUIREMENTS–

## STUDENT THROUGH ATP

## Student Pilots License and Medical Certificate.

**When do I need a medical certificate?** You need a medical certificate before flying solo in an airplane. It is suggested that you get your medical certificate before beginning flight training. This will alert you to any medical condition that would prevent you from becoming a pilot before you pay for lessons.

**How do I get a medical certificate?** By passing a physical examination administered by a doctor who is an FAA-authorized aviation medical examiner.

**Where do I get my medical certificate?** From any FAA-authorized aviation medical examiner. There are approximately 6,000 of them in the U.S.

**Where can I get a list of FAA-authorized aviation medical examiners?**

The FAA publishes a directory that lists them by name and address. Your flight school or instructor should also be able to supply this information.

You can also go to: http://www.faa.gov/pilots/ame locator.

When required, what class of medical certificate must a student pilot have? **Third-class, although any class will suffice. Medical certificates are designated as first-class, second-class, or third-class. Generally, first-class is designed for the airline transport pilot; second-class for the commercial pilot; and third-class for the student, recreational and private pilot.**

**If I have a physical disability, can I get a medical certificate?**
Yes. Medical certificates can be issued in many cases where physical disabilities are involved. Depending on the nature of the disability, you may have some operating limitations. If you have any questions, contact an FAA-authorized aviation medical examiner before beginning flight training.

**Must I carry my medical certificate when I am flying solo?**
Yes.

**When do I need a student pilot certificate?** Before you can fly solo. You don't need a student pilot certificate to take flying lessons.

**Am I eligible for a student pilot certificate?**
You are eligible if:

- You are at least 16 years old. If you plan to pilot a glider or balloon, you must be at least 14 years old.
- You can read, speak, and understand English AND
- You hold at least a current third-class medical certificate

**How do I get a student pilot certificate?**

Upon your request, an FAA-authorized aviation medical examiner will issue you a combined medical certificate and Student Pilot Certificate after you complete your physical examination. Applicants who fail to meet certain requirements or who have physical disabilities which might limit, but not prevent, their acting as pilots, should contact the nearest FAA office.

**How long are my student pilot certificate and my medical certificate valid?** A student pilot certificate expires 24 calendar months from the month in which it is issued. A third class medical certificate expires:

- If under age 40 on the date of examination, at the end of the last day of the 60th month after the month after the date of examination.
- If age 40 or older on the date of examination, at the end of the last day of the 24th month after the month after the date of examination.

**Should my flight instructor endorse my student pilot certificate before or after my first solo flight?** Before the solo flight. The endorsement certifies that you are competent to solo.

**If I solo in more than one make or model of aircraft, must I have an endorsement for each on my student pilot certificate? If so, who should endorse the certificate?** Yes. Your flight instructor must make this endorsement before you solo in each make or model of aircraft.

**Does the endorsement to solo allow me to make solo cross-country flights?** No. You also have to get a cross-country flight endorsement from you flight instructor.

**Must I carry my student pilot certificate with me when I am piloting an aircraft in solo flight?** Yes.

## Private Pilot Requirements

To be eligible for a private pilot certificate, a person must:

(a) Be at least 17 years of age for a rating in other than a glider or balloon.

(b) Be at least 16 years of age for a rating in a glider or balloon.

(c) Be able to read, speak, write, and understand the English language. If the applicant is unable to meet one of these requirements due to medical reasons, then the Administrator may place such operating limitations on that applicant's pilot certificate as are necessary for the safe operation of the aircraft.

(d) Receive a logbook endorsement from an authorized instructor who:

(1) Conducted the training or reviewed the person's home study on the aeronautical knowledge areas listed in Sec. 61.105(b) of this part that apply to the aircraft rating sought; and

(2) Certified that the person is prepared for the required knowledge test.

(e) Pass the required knowledge test on the aeronautical knowledge areas listed in Sec. 61.105(b) of this part.

(f) Receive flight training and a logbook endorsement from an authorized instructor who:

(1) Conducted the training in the areas of operation listed in Sec. 61.107(b) of this part that apply to the aircraft rating sought; and

(2) Certified that the person is prepared for the required practical test.

(g) Meet the aeronautical experience requirements of this part that apply to the aircraft rating sought before applying for the practical test.

(h) Pass a practical test on the areas of operation listed in Sec. 61.107(b) of this part that apply to the aircraft rating sought.

(i) Comply with the appropriate sections of this part that apply to the aircraft category and class rating sought.

## Aeronautical knowledge.

(a) General. A person who is applying for a private pilot certificate must receive and log ground training from an authorized instructor or complete a home-study course on the aeronautical knowledge areas of paragraph (b) of this section that apply to the aircraft category and class rating sought.

(b) Aeronautical knowledge areas.

(1) Applicable Federal Aviation Regulations of this chapter that relate to private pilot privileges, limitations, and flight operations;

(2) Accident reporting requirements of the National Transportation Safety Board;

(3) Use of the applicable portions of the "Aeronautical Information Manual" and FAA advisory circulars;

(4) Use of aeronautical charts for VFR navigation using pilotage, dead reckoning, and navigation systems;

(5) Radio communication procedures;

(6) Recognition of critical weather situations from the ground and in flight, windshear avoidance, and the procurement and use of aeronautical weather reports and forecasts;

(7) Safe and efficient operation of aircraft, including collision avoidance, and recognition and avoidance of wake turbulence;
(8) Effects of density altitude on takeoff and climb performance;
(9) Weight and balance computations;
(10) Principles of aerodynamics, powerplants, and aircraft systems;
(11) Stall awareness, spin entry, spins, and spin recovery techniques for the airplane and glider category ratings;
(12) Aeronautical decision making and judgment; and
(13) Preflight action that includes--
(i) How to obtain information on runway lengths at airports of intended use, data on takeoff and landing distances, weather reports and forecasts, and fuel requirements; and
(ii) How to plan for alternatives if the planned flight cannot be completed or delays are encountered.

## Private Pilot Flight Proficiency
### Flight proficiency.
(a) General. A person who applies for a private pilot certificate must receive and log ground and flight training from an authorized instructor on the areas of operation of this section that apply to the aircraft category and class rating sought.
(b) Areas of operation. (1) For an airplane category rating with a single-engine class rating: (i) Preflight preparation;
(ii) Preflight procedures;
(iii) Airport and seaplane base operations;
(iv) Takeoffs, landings, and go-arounds;
(v) Performance maneuvers;
(vi) Ground reference maneuvers;
(vii) Navigation;
(viii) Slow flight and stalls;
(ix) Basic instrument maneuvers;
(x) Emergency operations;
(xi) Night operations, except as provided in Sec. 61.110 of this part; and

(xii) Postflight procedures.

## Private Pilot Aeronautical Experience
### Aeronautical experience.

(a) For an airplane single-engine rating. Except as provided in paragraph (i) of this section, a person who applies for a private pilot certificate with an airplane category and single-engine class rating must log at least 40 hours of flight time that includes at least 20 hours of flight training from an authorized instructor and 10 hours of solo flight training in the areas of operation listed in Sec. 61.107(b)(1) of this part, and the training must include at least--

(1) 3 hours of cross-country flight training in a single-engine airplane;

(2) Except as provided in Sec. 61.110 of this part, 3 hours of night flight training in a single-engine airplane that includes--

(i) One cross-country flight of over 100 nautical miles total distance; and

(ii) 10 takeoffs and 10 landings to a full stop (with each landing involving a flight in the traffic pattern) at an airport.

(3) 3 hours of flight training in a single-engine airplane on the control and maneuvering of an airplane solely by reference to instruments, including straight and level flight, constant airspeed climbs and descents, turns to a heading, recovery from unusual flight attitudes, radio communications, and the use of navigation systems/facilities and radar services appropriate to instrument flight;

(4) 3 hours of flight training in preparation for the practical test in a single-engine airplane, which must have been performed within 60 days preceding the date of the test; and

(5) 10 hours of solo flight time in a single-engine airplane, consisting of at least--

(i) 5 hours of solo cross-country time;

(ii) One solo cross-country flight of at least 150 nautical miles total distance, with full-stop landings at a minimum of three points, and one segment of the flight consisting of a straight-line distance of at least 50 nautical miles between the takeoff and landing locations; and

(iii) Three takeoffs and three landings to a full stop (with each landing involving a flight in the traffic pattern) at an airport with an operating control tower.

# Instrument Rating Requirements

(a) *General.* A person who applies for an instrument rating must:

(1) Hold at least a private pilot certificate with an airplane, helicopter, or powered-lift rating appropriate to the instrument rating sought;

(2) Be able to read, speak, write, and understand the English language. If the applicant is unable to meet any of these requirements due to a medical condition, the Administrator may place such operating limitations on the applicant's pilot certificate as are necessary for the safe operation of the aircraft;

(3) Receive and log ground training from an authorized instructor or accomplish a home-study course of training on the aeronautical knowledge areas of paragraph (b) of this section that apply to the instrument rating sought;

(4) Receive a logbook or training record endorsement from an authorized instructor certifying that the person is prepared to take the required knowledge test;

(5) Receive and log training on the areas of operation of paragraph (c) of this section from an authorized instructor in an aircraft, flight simulator, or flight training device that represents an airplane, helicopter, or powered-lift appropriate to the instrument rating sought;

(6) Receive a logbook or training record endorsement from an authorized instructor certifying that the person is prepared to take the required practical test;

(7) Pass the required knowledge test on the aeronautical knowledge areas of paragraph (b) of this section; however, an applicant is not required to take another knowledge test when that person already holds an instrument rating; and

(8) Pass the required practical test on the areas of operation in paragraph (c) of this section in—

(i) An airplane, helicopter, or powered-lift appropriate to the rating sought; or

(ii) A flight simulator or a flight training device appropriate to the rating sought and for the specific maneuver or instrument approach procedure performed. If an approved flight training device is used for the practical test, the instrument approach procedures conducted in that flight training device are limited to one precision and one nonprecision approach, provided the flight training device is approved for the procedure performed.

(b) *Aeronautical knowledge.* A person who applies for an instrument rating must have received and logged ground training from an authorized instructor or accomplished a home-study course on the following aeronautical knowledge areas that apply to the instrument rating sought:

(1) Federal Aviation Regulations of this chapter that apply to flight operations under IFR;

(2) Appropriate information that applies to flight operations under IFR in the "Aeronautical Information Manual;"

(3) Air traffic control system and procedures for instrument flight operations;

(4) IFR navigation and approaches by use of navigation systems;

(5) Use of IFR en route and instrument approach procedure charts;

(6) Procurement and use of aviation weather reports and forecasts and the elements of forecasting weather trends based on that information and personal observation of weather conditions;

(7) Safe and efficient operation of aircraft under instrument flight rules and conditions;

(8) Recognition of critical weather situations and windshear avoidance;

(9) Aeronautical decision making and judgment; and

(10) Crew resource management, including crew communication and coordination.

(c) *Flight proficiency.* A person who applies for an instrument rating must receive and log training from an authorized

instructor in an aircraft, or in a flight simulator or flight training device, in accordance with paragraph (e) of this section, that includes the following areas of operation:
(1) Preflight preparation;
(2) Preflight procedures;
(3) Air traffic control clearances and procedures;
(4) Flight by reference to instruments;
(5) Navigation systems;
(6) Instrument approach procedures;
(7) Emergency operations; and
(8) Postflight procedures.
(d) *Aeronautical experience for the instrument-airplane rating.* A person who applies for an instrument-airplane rating must have logged:
(1) Fifty hours of cross country flight time as pilot in command, of which 10 hours must have been in an airplane; and
(2) Forty hours of actual or simulated instrument time in the areas of operation listed in paragraph (c) of this section, of which 15 hours must have been received from an authorized instructor who holds an instrument-airplane rating, and the instrument time includes:
(i) Three hours of instrument flight training from an authorized instructor in an airplane that is appropriate to the instrument-airplane rating within 2 calendar months before the date of the practical test; and
(ii) Instrument flight training on cross country flight procedures, including one cross country flight in an airplane with an authorized instructor, that is performed under instrument flight rules, when a flight plan has been filed with an air traffic control facility, and that involves—
(A) A flight of 250 nautical miles along airways or by directed routing from an air traffic control facility;
(B) An instrument approach at each airport; and
(C) Three different kinds of approaches with the use of navigation systems.
(e) *Aeronautical experience for the instrument-helicopter rating.* A person who applies for an instrument-helicopter rating must have logged:

(1) Fifty hours of cross country flight time as pilot in command, of which 10 hours must have been in a helicopter; and

(2) Forty hours of actual or simulated instrument time in the areas of operation listed under paragraph (c) of this section, of which 15 hours must have been with an authorized instructor who holds an instrument-helicopter rating, and the instrument time includes:

(i) Three hours of instrument flight training from an authorized instructor in a helicopter that is appropriate to the instrument-helicopter rating within 2 calendar months before the date of the practical test; and

(ii) Instrument flight training on cross country flight procedures, including one cross country flight in a helicopter with an authorized instructor that is performed under instrument flight rules and a flight plan has been filed with an air traffic control facility, and involves—

(A) A flight of 100 nautical miles along airways or by directed routing from an air traffic control facility;

(B) An instrument approach at each airport; and

(C) Three different kinds of approaches with the use of navigation systems.

(f) *Aeronautical experience for the instrument-powered-lift rating.* A person who applies for an instrument-powered-lift rating must have logged:

(1) Fifty hours of cross country flight time as pilot in command, of which 10 hours cross country must have been in a powered-lift; and

(2) Forty hours of actual or simulated instrument time in the areas of operation listed under paragraph (c) of this section, of which 15 hours must have been received from an authorized instructor who holds an instrument-powered-lift rating, and the instrument time includes:

(i) Three hours of instrument flight training from an authorized instructor in a powered-lift that is appropriate to the instrument-powered-lift rating within 2 calendar months before the date of the practical test; and

(ii) Instrument flight training on cross country flight procedures, including one cross country flight in a powered-lift with an authorized instructor that is performed under instrument flight rules, when a flight plan has been filed with an air traffic control facility, that involves—

(A) A flight of 250 nautical miles along airways or by directed routing from an air traffic control facility;

(B) An instrument approach at each airport; and

(C) Three different kinds of approaches with the use of navigation systems.

(g) *Use of flight simulators or flight training devices.* If the instrument time was provided by an authorized instructor in a flight simulator or flight training device—

(1) A maximum of 30 hours may be performed in that flight simulator or flight training device if the instrument time was completed in accordance with part 142 of this chapter; or

(2) A maximum of 20 hours may be performed in that flight simulator or flight training device if the instrument time was not completed in accordance with part 142 of this chapter.

(h) *Use of an aviation training device.* A maximum of 10 hours of instrument time received in an aviation training device may be credited for the instrument time requirements of this section if—

(1) The device is approved and authorized by the FAA;

(2) An authorized instructor provides the instrument time in the device;

(3) No more than 10 hours of instrument time in a flight simulator or flight training device was credited for the instrument time requirements of this section;

(4) A view-limiting device was worn by the applicant when logging instrument time in the device; and

(5) The FAA approved the instrument training and instrument tasks performed in the device.

# Commercial Pilot Requirements

To be eligible for a commercial pilot certificate, a person must:

(a) Be at least 18 years of age;

(b) Be able to read, speak, write, and understand the English language. If the applicant is unable to meet one of these requirements due to medical reasons, then the Administrator may place such operating limitations on that applicant's pilot certificate as are necessary for the safe operation of the aircraft.

(c) Receive a logbook endorsement from an authorized instructor who:

(1) Conducted the required ground training or reviewed the person's home study on the aeronautical knowledge areas listed in §61.125 of this part that apply to the aircraft category and class rating sought; and

(2) Certified that the person is prepared for the required knowledge test that applies to the aircraft category and class rating sought.

(d) Pass the required knowledge test on the aeronautical knowledge areas listed in §61.125 of this part;

(e) Receive the required training and a logbook endorsement from an authorized instructor who:

(1) Conducted the training on the areas of operation listed in §61.127(b) of this part that apply to the aircraft category and class rating sought; and

(2) Certified that the person is prepared for the required practical test.

(f) Meet the aeronautical experience requirements of this subpart that apply to the aircraft category and class rating sought before applying for the practical test;

(g) Pass the required practical test on the areas of operation listed in §61.127(b) of this part that apply to the aircraft category and class rating sought;

(h) Hold at least a private pilot certificate issued under this part or meet the requirements of §61.73; and

(i) Comply with the sections of this part that apply to the aircraft category and class rating sought.

**Aeronautical knowledge.**

(a) *General.* A person who applies for a commercial pilot certificate must receive and log ground training from an authorized instructor, or complete a home-study course, on the aeronautical knowledge areas of paragraph (b) of this section that apply to the aircraft category and class rating sought.

(b) *Aeronautical knowledge areas.* (1) Applicable Federal Aviation Regulations of this chapter that relate to commercial pilot privileges, limitations, and flight operations;

(2) Accident reporting requirements of the National Transportation Safety Board;

(3) Basic aerodynamics and the principles of flight;

(4) Meteorology to include recognition of critical weather situations, windshear recognition and avoidance, and the use of aeronautical weather reports and forecasts;

(5) Safe and efficient operation of aircraft;

(6) Weight and balance computations;

(7) Use of performance charts;

(8) Significance and effects of exceeding aircraft performance limitations;

(9) Use of aeronautical charts and a magnetic compass for pilotage and dead reckoning;

(10) Use of air navigation facilities;

(11) Aeronautical decision making and judgment;

(12) Principles and functions of aircraft systems;

(13) Maneuvers, procedures, and emergency operations appropriate to the aircraft;

(14) Night and high-altitude operations;

(15) Procedures for operating within the National Airspace System; and

(16) Procedures for flight and ground training for lighter-than-air ratings.

**Flight proficiency.**

(a) *General.* A person who applies for a commercial pilot certificate must receive and log ground and flight training from an authorized instructor on the areas of operation of this section that apply to the aircraft category and class rating sought.

(b) *Areas of operation.* (1) For an airplane category rating with a single-engine class rating:

(i) Preflight preparation;

(ii) Preflight procedures;

(iii) Airport and seaplane base operations;

(iv) Takeoffs, landings, and go-arounds;

(v) Performance maneuvers;

(vi) Ground reference maneuvers;

(vii) Navigation;

(viii) Slow flight and stalls;

(ix) Emergency operations;

(x) High-altitude operations; and

(xi) Postflight procedures.

(2) For an airplane category rating with a multiengine class rating:

(i) Preflight preparation;

(ii) Preflight procedures;

(iii) Airport and seaplane base operations;

(iv) Takeoffs, landings, and go-arounds;

(v) Performance maneuvers;

(vi) Navigation;

(vii) Slow flight and stalls;

(viii) Emergency operations;

(ix) Multiengine operations;

(x) High-altitude operations; and

(xi) Postflight procedures.

## Aeronautical experience.

(a) *For an airplane single-engine rating.* Except as provided in paragraph (i) of this section, a person who applies for a commercial pilot certificate with an airplane category and single-engine class rating must log at least 250 hours of flight time as a pilot that consists of at least:

(1) 100 hours in powered aircraft, of which 50 hours must be in airplanes.

(2) 100 hours of pilot-in-command flight time, which includes at least—

(i) 50 hours in airplanes; and

(ii) 50 hours in cross-country flight of which at least 10 hours must be in airplanes.

(3) 20 hours of training on the areas of operation listed in §61.127(b)(1) of this part that includes at least—

(i) Ten hours of instrument training using a view-limiting device including attitude instrument flying, partial panel skills, recovery from unusual flight attitudes, and intercepting and tracking navigational systems. Five hours of the 10 hours required on instrument training must be in a single engine airplane;

(ii) 10 hours of training in an airplane that has a retractable landing gear, flaps, and a controllable pitch propeller, or is turbine-powered, or for an applicant seeking a single-engine seaplane rating, 10 hours of training in a seaplane that has flaps and a controllable pitch propeller;

(iii) One 2-hour cross country flight in a single engine airplane in daytime conditions that consists of a total straight-line distance of more than 100 nautical miles from the original point of departure;

(iv) One 2-hour cross country flight in a single engine airplane in nighttime conditions that consists of a total straight-line distance of more than 100 nautical miles from the original point of departure; and

(v) Three hours in a single-engine airplane with an authorized instructor in preparation for the practical test within the preceding 2 calendar months from the month of the test.

(4) Ten hours of solo flight time in a single engine airplane or 10 hours of flight time performing the duties of pilot in command in a single engine airplane with an authorized instructor on board (either of which may be credited towards the flight time requirement under paragraph (a)(2) of this section), on the areas of operation listed under §61.127(b)(1) that include—

(i) One cross-country flight of not less than 300 nautical miles total distance, with landings at a minimum of three points, one of which is a straight-line distance of at least 250 nautical miles from the original departure point. However, if this requirement is being met in Hawaii, the longest segment need only have a straight-line distance of at least 150 nautical miles; and

(ii) 5 hours in night VFR conditions with 10 takeoffs and 10 landings (with each landing involving a flight in the traffic pattern) at an airport with an operating control tower.

(b) *For an airplane multiengine rating.* Except as provided in paragraph (i) of this section, a person who applies for a commercial pilot certificate with an airplane category and multiengine class rating must log at least 250 hours of flight time as a pilot that consists of at least:

(1) 100 hours in powered aircraft, of which 50 hours must be in airplanes.

(2) 100 hours of pilot-in-command flight time, which includes at least—

(i) 50 hours in airplanes; and

(ii) 50 hours in cross-country flight of which at least 10 hours must be in airplanes.

(3) 20 hours of training on the areas of operation listed in §61.127(b)(2) of this part that includes at least—

(i) Ten hours of instrument training using a view-limiting device including attitude instrument flying, partial panel skills, recovery from unusual flight attitudes, and intercepting and tracking navigational systems. Five hours of the 10 hours required on instrument training must be in a multiengine airplane;

(ii) 10 hours of training in a multiengine airplane that has a retractable landing gear, flaps, and controllable pitch propellers, or is turbine-powered, or for an applicant seeking a multiengine seaplane rating, 10 hours of training in a multiengine seaplane that has flaps and a controllable pitch propeller;

(iii) One 2-hour cross country flight in a multiengine airplane in daytime conditions that consists of a total straight-line distance of more than 100 nautical miles from the original point of departure;

(iv) One 2-hour cross country flight in a multiengine airplane in nighttime conditions that consists of a total straight-line distance of more than 100 nautical miles from the original point of departure; and

(v) Three hours in a multiengine airplane with an authorized instructor in preparation for the practical test within the preceding 2 calendar months from the month of the test.

(4) 10 hours of solo flight time in a multiengine airplane or 10 hours of flight time performing the duties of pilot in command in a multiengine airplane with an authorized instructor (either of which may be credited towards the flight time requirement in paragraph (b)(2) of this section), on the areas of operation listed in §61.127(b)(2) of this part that includes at least—

(i) One cross-country flight of not less than 300 nautical miles total distance with landings at a minimum of three points, one of which is a straight-line distance of at least 250 nautical miles from the original departure point. However, if this requirement is being met in Hawaii, the longest segment need only have a straight-line distance of at least 150 nautical miles; and

(ii) 5 hours in night VFR conditions with 10 takeoffs and 10 landings (with each landing involving a flight with a traffic pattern) at an airport with an operating control tower.

# Airline Transport Pilot Requirements

To be eligible for an airline transport pilot certificate, a person must:
(a) Be at least 23 years of age;
(b) Be able to read, speak, write, and understand the English language. If the applicant is unable to meet one of these requirements due to medical reasons, then the Administrator may place such operating limitations on that applicant's pilot certificate as are necessary for the safe operation of the aircraft;
(c) Be of good moral character;
(d) Meet at least one of the following requirements:
(1) Holds a commercial pilot certificate with an instrument rating issued under this part;
(2) Meet the military experience requirements under §61.73 of this part to qualify for a commercial pilot certificate, and an instrument rating if the person is a rated military pilot or former rated military pilot of an Armed Force of the United States; or
(3) Holds either a foreign airline transport pilot license with instrument privileges, or a foreign commercial pilot license with an instrument rating, that—
(i) Was issued by a contracting State to the Convention on International Civil Aviation; and
(ii) Contains no geographical limitations.
(e) Meet the aeronautical experience requirements of this subpart that apply to the aircraft category and class rating sought before applying for the practical test;
(f) Pass a knowledge test on the aeronautical knowledge areas of §61.155(c) of this part that apply to the aircraft category and class rating sought;
(g) Pass the practical test on the areas of operation listed in §61.157(e) of this part that apply to the aircraft category and class rating sought; and
(h) Comply with the sections of this subpart that apply to the aircraft category and class rating sought.
**Aeronautical knowledge.**
(a) *General.* The knowledge test for an airline transport pilot certificate is based on the aeronautical knowledge areas

listed in paragraph (c) of this section that are appropriate to the aircraft category and class rating sought.

(b) *Aircraft type rating.* A person who is applying for an additional aircraft type rating to be added to an airline transport pilot certificate is not required to pass a knowledge test if that person's airline transport pilot certificate lists the aircraft category and class rating that is appropriate to the type rating sought.

(c) *Aeronautical knowledge areas.* (1) Applicable Federal Aviation Regulations of this chapter that relate to airline transport pilot privileges, limitations, and flight operations;

(2) Meteorology, including knowledge of and effects of fronts, frontal characteristics, cloud formations, icing, and upper-air data;

(3) General system of weather and NOTAM collection, dissemination, interpretation, and use;

(4) Interpretation and use of weather charts, maps, forecasts, sequence reports, abbreviations, and symbols;

(5) National Weather Service functions as they pertain to operations in the National Airspace System;

(6) Windshear and microburst awareness, identification, and avoidance;

(7) Principles of air navigation under instrument meteorological conditions in the National Airspace System;

(8) Air traffic control procedures and pilot responsibilities as they relate to en route operations, terminal area and radar operations, and instrument departure and approach procedures;

(9) Aircraft loading, weight and balance, use of charts, graphs, tables, formulas, and computations, and their effect on aircraft performance;

(10) Aerodynamics relating to an aircraft's flight characteristics and performance in normal and abnormal flight regimes;

(11) Human factors;

(12) Aeronautical decision making and judgment; and

(13) Crew resource management to include crew communication and coordination.

**Flight proficiency.**

(a) *General.* (1) The practical test for an airline transport pilot certificate is given for—

(i) An airplane category and single engine class rating.

(ii) An airplane category and multiengine class rating.

(iii) A rotorcraft category and helicopter class rating.

(iv) A powered-lift category rating.

(v) An aircraft type rating.

(2) A person who is applying for an airline transport pilot practical test must meet—

(i) The eligibility requirements of §61.153; and

(ii) The aeronautical knowledge and aeronautical experience requirements of this subpart that apply to the aircraft category and class rating sought.

(b) *Aircraft type rating.* Except as provided in paragraph (c) of this section, a person who applies for an aircraft type rating to be added to an airline transport pilot certificate or applies for a type rating to be concurrently completed with an airline transport pilot certificate:

(1) Must receive and log ground and flight training from an authorized instructor on the areas of operation under this section that apply to the aircraft type rating;

(2) Must receive a logbook endorsement from an authorized instructor that certifies the applicant completed the training on the areas of operation listed under paragraph (e) of this section that apply to the aircraft type rating; and

(3) Must perform the practical test in actual or simulated instrument conditions, except as provided under paragraph (g) of this section.

(c) *Exceptions.* A person who applies for an aircraft type rating to be added to an airline transport pilot certificate or an aircraft type rating concurrently with an airline transport pilot certificate, and who is an employee of a certificate holder operating under part 121 or part 135 of this chapter, does not need to comply with the requirements of paragraph (b) of this section if the applicant presents a training record that shows completion of that certificate holder's approved pilot in command training program for the aircraft type rating.

(d) *Upgrading type ratings.* Any type rating(s) and limitations on a pilot certificate of an applicant who completes an airline transport pilot practical test will be included at the airline transport pilot certification level, provided the applicant passes the practical test in the same category and class of aircraft for which the applicant holds the type rating(s).

(e) *Areas of operation.* (1) For an airplane category—single engine class rating:

(i) Preflight preparation;

(ii) Preflight procedures;

(iii) Takeoff and departure phase;

(iv) In-flight maneuvers;

(v) Instrument procedures;

(vi) Landings and approaches to landings;

(vii) Normal and abnormal procedures;

(viii) Emergency procedures; and

(ix) Postflight procedures.

(2) For an airplane category—multiengine class rating:

(i) Preflight preparation;

(ii) Preflight procedures;

(iii) Takeoff and departure phase;

(iv) In-flight maneuvers;

(v) Instrument procedures;

(vi) Landings and approaches to landings;

(vii) Normal and abnormal procedures;

(viii) Emergency procedures; and

(ix) Postflight procedures.

(3) For a powered-lift category rating:

(i) Preflight preparation;

(ii) Preflight procedures;

(iii) Takeoff and departure phase;

(iv) In-flight maneuvers;

(v) Instrument procedures;

(vi) Landings and approaches to landings;

(vii) Normal and abnormal procedures;

(viii) Emergency procedures; and

(ix) Postflight procedures.

 (f) *Proficiency and competency checks conducted under part 121, part 135, or subpart K of part 91.* (1) Successful completion of any of the following checks satisfies the flight proficiency requirements of this section for the issuance of an airline transport pilot certificate and/or the appropriate aircraft rating:

(i) A proficiency check under §121.441 of this chapter.

(ii) Both a competency check under §135.293(a)(2) and §135.293(b) of this chapter and pilot-in-command instrument proficiency check under §135.297 of this chapter.

(iii) Both a competency check under §91.1065 of this chapter and a pilot-in-command instrument proficiency check under §91.1069 of this chapter.

(2) The checks specified in paragraph (f)(1) of this section must be conducted by one of the following:

(i) An FAA Aviation Safety Inspector.

(ii) An Aircrew Program Designee who is authorized to perform proficiency and/or competency checks for the air carrier whose approved training program has been satisfactorily completed by the pilot applicant.

(iii) A Training Center Evaluator with appropriate certification authority who is also authorized to perform the portions of the competency and/or proficiency checks required by paragraph (f)(1) of this section for maneuvers and procedures required on the practical test under the following circumstances—

(1) The rating is limited to "VFR only."

(2) The type rating is added to an airline transport pilot certificate that has instrument privileges in that category and class of aircraft.

(3) The "VFR only" limitation may be removed for that aircraft type after the applicant:

(i) Passes a practical test in that type of aircraft on the appropriate instrument maneuvers and procedures in §61.157; or

(ii) Becomes qualified in §61.73(d) for that type of aircraft.

(h) *Multiengine airplane with a single-pilot station.* An applicant for a type rating, at the ATP certification level, in a multiengine airplane with a single-pilot station must perform the practical test in the multi-seat version of that airplane. The practical test may be performed in the single-seat version of that airplane if the Examiner is in a position to observe the applicant during the practical test in the case where there is no multi-seat version of that multiengine airplane.

(i) *Single engine airplane with a single-pilot station.* An applicant for a type rating, at the ATP certification level, in a single engine airplane with a single-pilot station must perform the practical test in the multi-seat version of that single engine airplane. The practical test may be performed in the single-seat version of that airplane if the Examiner is in a position to observe the applicant during the practical test in the case where there is no multi-seat version of that single engine airplane.

(j) *Waiver authority.* An Examiner who conducts a practical test may waive any task for which the FAA has provided waiver authority.

### Aeronautical experience: Airplane category rating.

(a) Except as provided in paragraphs (b), (c), and (d) of this section, a person who is applying for an airline transport pilot certificate with an airplane category and class rating must have at least 1,500 hours of total time as a pilot that includes at least:

(1) 500 hours of cross-country flight time.

(2) 100 hours of night flight time.

(3) 75 hours of instrument flight time, in actual or simulated instrument conditions, subject to the following:

(i) Except as provided in paragraph (a)(3)(ii) of this section, an applicant may not receive credit for more than a total of 25 hours of simulated instrument time in a flight simulator or flight training device.

(ii) A maximum of 50 hours of training in a flight simulator or flight training device may be credited toward the instrument flight time requirements of paragraph (a)(3) of this section if the training was accomplished in a course conducted by a training center certificated under part 142 of this chapter.

(iii) Training in a flight simulator or flight training device must be accomplished in a flight simulator or flight training device, representing an airplane.

(4) 250 hours of flight time in an airplane as a pilot in command, or as second in command performing the duties of pilot in command while under the supervision of a pilot in

command, or any combination thereof, which includes at least—

(i) 100 hours of cross-country flight time; and

(ii) 25 hours of night flight time.

(5) Not more than 100 hours of the total aeronautical experience requirements of paragraph (a) of this section may be obtained in a flight simulator or flight training device that represents an airplane, provided the aeronautical experience was obtained in an approved course conducted by a training center certificated under part 142 of this chapter.

(b) A person who has performed at least 20 night takeoffs and landings to a full stop may substitute each additional night takeoff and landing to a full stop for 1 hour of night flight time to satisfy the requirements of paragraph (a)(2) of this section; however, not more than 25 hours of night flight time may be credited in this manner.

(c) A commercial pilot may credit the following second-in-command flight time or flight-engineer flight time toward the 1,500 hours of total time as a pilot required by paragraph (a) of this section:

(1) Second-in-command time, provided the time is acquired in an airplane—

(i) Required to have more than one pilot flight crewmember by the airplane's flight manual, type certificate, or the regulations under which the flight is being conducted;

(ii) Engaged in operations under subpart K of part 91, part 121, or part 135 of this chapter for which a second in command is required; or

(iii) That is required by the operating rules of this chapter to have more than one pilot flight crewmember.

(2) Flight-engineer time, provided the time—

(i) Is acquired in an airplane required to have a flight engineer by the airplane's flight manual or type certificate;

(ii) Is acquired while engaged in operations under part 121 of this chapter for which a flight engineer is required;

(iii) Is acquired while the person is participating in a pilot training program approved under part 121 of this chapter; and

(iv) Does not exceed more than 1 hour for each 3 hours of flight engineer flight time for a total credited time of no more than 500 hours.

(3) Flight-engineer time, provided the flight time—

(i) Is acquired as a U.S. Armed Forces' flight engineer crewmember in an airplane that requires a flight engineer crewmember by the flight manual;

(ii) Is acquired while the person is participating in a flight engineer crewmember training program for the U.S. Armed Forces; and

(iii) Does not exceed 1 hour for each 3 hours of flight engineer flight time for a total credited time of no more than 500 hours.

(d) An applicant is issued an airline transport pilot certificate with the limitation, "Holder does not meet the pilot in command aeronautical experience requirements of ICAO," as prescribed under Article 39 of the Convention on International Civil Aviation, if the applicant does not meet the ICAO requirements contained in Annex 1 "Personnel Licensing" to the Convention on International Civil Aviation, but otherwise meets the aeronautical experience requirements of this section.

(e) An applicant is entitled to an airline transport pilot certificate without the ICAO limitation specified under paragraph (d) of this section when the applicant presents satisfactory evidence of having met the ICAO requirements under paragraph (d) of this section and otherwise meets the aeronautical experience requirements of this section.

# CHAPTER 15

## PILOT PAY RATES

*Pilot pay scales are constantly changing due to union contracts and various other factors. The information below is intended to provide approximate salary information. Current information can often be found on the various employer websites.

## Major Airline Pay Scales

### Airtran Airlines
First Year Pay – First Officer = $41,000
Fifth Year Pay – First Officer = $87,000
Tenth Year Pay – Captain = $149,000
Max Pay – Captain = $157,000

### Alaska Airlines
First Year Pay – First Officer = $46,000
Fifth Year Pay – First Officer = $100,000
Tenth Year Pay – Captain = $167,000
Max Pay – Captain = $173,000

### American Airlines
First Year Pay – First Officer = $34,000

Fifth Year Pay – First Officer  =  $95,000
Tenth Year Pay – Captain  =  $171,000
Max Pay – Captain  =  $204,000

### Delta Airlines
First Year Pay – First Officer  =  $59,000
Fifth Year Pay – First Officer  =  $122,000
Tenth Year Pay – Captain  =  $167,000
Max Pay – Captain  =  $245,000

### FedEx
First Year Pay – First Officer  =  $59,000
Fifth Year Pay – First Officer  =  $123,000
Tenth Year Pay – Captain  =  $198,000
Max Pay – Captain  =  $243,000

### JetBlue
First Year Pay – First Officer  =  $45,000
Fifth Year Pay – First Officer  =  $88,000
Tenth Year Pay – Captain  =  $134,000
Max Pay – Captain  =  $152,000

### Southwest Airlines
First Year Pay – First Officer  =  $55,000
Fifth Year Pay – First Officer  =  $124,000
Tenth Year Pay – Captain  =  $201,000
Max Pay – Captain  =  $206,000

### United Airlines
First Year Pay – First Officer  =  $58,000
Fifth Year Pay – First Officer  =  $131,000
Tenth Year Pay – Captain  =  $171,000
Max Pay – Captain  =  $225,000

## UPS
First Year Pay – First Officer = $34,000
Fifth Year Pay – First Officer = $129,000
Tenth Year Pay – Captain = $218,000
Max Pay – Captain = $228,000

## US Airways
First Year Pay – First Officer = $40,000
Fifth Year Pay – First Officer = $83,000
Tenth Year Pay – Captain = $91,000
Max Pay – Captain = $153,000

### Regional Jet Captains
Average – $93,000

### Regional Jet First Officers
Average - $43,000

### Regional Turboprop Captains
Average - $68,000

### Regional Turboprop First Officers
Average - $38,000

# Corporate Pilot Examples

### Boeing 737 / BBJ
Average Captain - $190,000

### Gulfstream IV Captain
Average - $133,000

## Learjet 35 Captain
Average - $77,000

## King Air 200
Average - $70,000

# CHAPTER 16

## COLLEGE AVIATION PROGRAMS

## College Aviation Programs

*This list is not all inclusive. New aviation programs start each year at both 2 and four year colleges.

### Arizona State University

Public School    Number of Aircraft: 18
Program: Professional Pilot
www.eastair.poly.asu.edu

### Auburn University

Public School    Number of Aircraft: 14
Program: Professional Flight Management
www.business.auburn.edu

### Bob Jones University

Private School    Number of Aircraft: 7
Program: Business and Commercial Aviation
www.bju.edu

## Delaware State University
Public School    Number of Aircraft: 10
Program: Professional Pilot
www.desu.edu

## Delta State University
Public School    Number of Aircraft: 21
Program: Bachelor of Commercial Aviation - Flight Operations
or Management
www.deltastate.edu

## Embry Riddle Aeronautical University - Daytona
Private School    Number of Aircraft: 88
Program: B.S. in Aeronautical Science
www.erau.edu/db/degrees

## Embry Riddle Aeronautical University - Prescott
Private School    Number of Aircraft: 23
Program: B.S. in Aeronautical Science
www.prescott.erau.edu

## Florida Institute of Technology
Private School    Number of Aircraft: 28
Program: Aeronautical Science
www.coa.fit.edu

## Hampton University
Private School    Number of Aircraft: 6
Program: BS in Flight Education
www.haptonu.edu

## Henderson State University
Private School    Number of Aircraft: 17
Program: BS in Aviation, Professional Pilot Track
www.hsu.edu/aviation

## Jacksonville University
Private School     Number of Aircraft: 10
Program: Aviation Management and Flight Operations
www.aviation.ju.edu

## Kansas State University at Salina
Public School     Number of Aircraft: 32
Program: BS in Aeronautical Technology-Professional Pilot
www.flyk-state.com

## Kent State University
Public School     Number of Aircraft: 25
Program: flight technology
www.kent.edu

## LeTourneau University
Private School     Number of Aircraft: 12
Program: school of aeronautical science
www.letu.edu

## Liberty University
Private School     Number of Aircraft: 15
Program: BS in Aeronautics
www.liberty.edu/aviation

## Louisiana Tech University
Public School     Number of Aircraft: 11
Program: Professional Aviation
www.latech.edu/aviation

## Marywood University
Private School     Number of Aircraft: seven
Program: BBA in Aviation Management
www.Marywood.edu

## Middle Georgia college
Public School     Number of Aircraft: 2
Program: BS in Professional Flight Management
www.mgc.edu/aviation

## Middle Tennessee State University
Public School    Number of Aircraft: 31
Program: BS in Aerospace with Professional Pilot
Concentration
www.mtsu.edu/aerospace

## Mountain State University
Private School    Number of Aircraft: 0
Program: BS in Airline Transport Professional Pilot Operations
www.atpdegree.com

## Rocky Mountain University
Private School    Number of Aircraft: 8
Program: Aeronautical Science
www.aviation.rocky.edu

## San Diego Christian College
Private School    Number of Aircraft: 8
Program: Bachelor of Science Aviation Technology
www.sdcc.edu/aviation

## Southeastern Oklahoma State University
Public School    Number of Aircraft: 10
Program: BS in Aviation, Professional Pilot Option
www.aviation.se.edu

## Southern Illinois University Carbondale
Public School    Number of Aircraft: 36
Program: AAS in Aviation Flight And BS in Aviation
Management
www.aviation.siu.edu

## Ohio State University
Public School    Number of Aircraft: 17
Program: Aircraft Systems - Professional Pilot
www.aviation.ohio-state.edu

## University of Alaska Anchorage

Public School    Number of Aircraft: 9
Program: BS in Aviation Technology - Professional Pilot
www.uaa.alaska.edu

## University of Central Missouri
Public School    Number of Aircraft: 9
Program: Bachelor BS In Technology - Professional Pilot Major
www.ucmo.edu.aviation

## University of Dubuque
Private School    Number of Aircraft: 23
Program: BS in Flight Operations with Airline Concentration
www.dbq.edu/aviation

## University of Illinois
Public School    Number of Aircraft: 30
Program: BS in Aviation Human Factors
www.aviation.illinois.edu

## University of Maryland Eastern Shore
Public School    Number of Aircraft: 0
Program: Aviation Sciences-Professional Pilot
www.umes.edu/aviation

## University of Oklahoma
Public School    Number of Aircraft: 22
Program: BS Professional Pilot and Aviation Management
www.aviation.ou.edu

## Utah State University
Public School    Number of Aircraft: 21
Program: BS in Aviation Technology-Professional Pilot
www.usu.edu

## University of North Dakota
Public School    Number of Aircraft: 21
Program: Bachelor of business ministration
www.aviation.und.edu

## Delta State University

Public School     Number of Aircraft: 21
Program: Bachelor of Commercial Aviation - Flight Operations
www.aviation.ohio-state.edu

# CHAPTER 17

## FLIGHT SCHOOL DIRECTORY

## Large National / Multi-Location Flight Schools

| Name | Website | Phone |
|---|---|---|
| AMERICAN FLYERS | www.americanflyers.net | 800-273-4954 |
| ATP – AIRLINE TRANSPORT PROFESSIONALS | www.atpflightschool.com | 800-255-2877 |
| FLIGHT SAFETY ACADEMY | www.flightsafetyacademy.com | 800-800-1411 |
| SPARTAN COLLEGE OF AERONAUTICS | www.spartan.edu | 800-331-1204 |

## Alabama

| Name | Address | Phone |
|---|---|---|
| ACCESSIBLE AVIATION INTERNATIONAL INC | 4243 EAST LAKE BLVD BIRMINGHAM, AL 35217 | (662)244-8434 |
| AUBURN UNIVERSITY | 700 AIRPORT ROAD AUBURN, AL 36830 | (334)844-5766 |

| | | |
|---|---|---|
| FLIGHT TRAINING OF MOBILE LLC | 23911 COUNTY ROAD 71 ROBERTSDALE, AL 36567 | (251)441-0723 |
| FLIGHT TRAINING OF MOBILE LLC | 2241 MICHIGAN AVENUE MOBILE, AL 36615 | (251)441-0723 |
| LIGHTNING AVIATION INC | 510 AIRPORT DRIVE FOLEY, AL 36535 | (251)943-5214 |
| SKYWARRIOR INC | 12301 AIRPORT ROAD BAY MINETTE, AL 36507 | (251)937-7957 |
| WALLACE STATE COMMUNITY COLLEGE | 231A COUNTRY RD. 1360 VINEMONT, AL 35179 | (256)737-3040 |

# Alaska

| Name | Address | Phone |
|---|---|---|
| ALYESKA HELICOPTERS LLC | 1740 EAST 5TH AVENUE ANCHORAGE, AK 99501 | (907)277-2007 |
| ELMENDORF AERO CLUB | HANGAR 7 PO BOX 6292 JBER, AK 99506 | (907)753-4167 |
| FLIGHT SAFETY ALASKA INC DBA: 1. LAND AND SEA AVIATION ALASKA LLC | 2400 E 5TH AVE SUITE #11 ANCHORAGE, AK 99501 | (907)274-2544 |
| GROUP 3 AVIATION INC | 2600 EAST 5TH AVE. ANCHORAGE, AK 99501 | (907)243-0147 |
| UNIVERSITY OF ALASKA ANCHORAGE | AVIATION PROFESSIONAL PILOT 2811 MERRILL FIELD DR | (907)786-7241 |

| | ANCHORAGE, AK 99501 | |
|---|---|---|
| YUUT YAQUNGVIAT LLC | PO BOX 2949<br>3341 NORTH APRON RD<br>BETHEL, AK 99559 | (907)543-7209 |

# Arizona

| Name | Address | Phone |
|---|---|---|
| AIRLINE TRAINING CENTER ARIZONA INC | 1658 S LITCHFIELD RD<br>GOODYEAR, AZ 85338 | (623)932-1700 |
| ARIZONA STATE UNIVERSITY DEPT OF AERONAUTICAL TECH | 7442 EAST TILLMAN AVENUE<br>MESA, AZ 85212 | (480)727-1024 |
| ARIZONA TYPE RATINGS | 26261 N. PASO TRAIL<br>SCOTTSDALE, AZ 85265 | (602)614-7994 |
| AVIATION PERFORMANCE SOLUTIONS LLC<br>DBA:<br>1. APS EMERGENCY MANEUVER TRAINING | 5865 S. SOSSAMAN ROAD<br>MESA, AZ 85212 | (480)279-1881 |
| BIRD ACQUISITION LLC | 2270 SOUTH AIRPORT DRIVE<br>SUITE 1<br>CHANDLER, AZ 85286 | (623)580-7900 |
| BIRD ACQUISITION LLC<br>DBA:<br>1. TRANSPAC AVIATION ACADEMY | 530 WEST DEER VALLEY RD. STE. 100<br>PHOENIX, AZ 85027 | (623)580-7961 |
| BIRD ACQUISITION LLC | 2270 SOUTH AIRPORT BLVD<br>SUITE #1<br>GLENDALE, AZ 85286 | (623)580-7695 |

| | | |
|---|---|---|
| BONESTEEL, JUNE | 14700 N. AIRPORT DR. SUITE 215 SCOTTSDALE, AZ 85260 | (602)569-0200 |
| CAE GLOBAL ACADEMY PHOENIX INC | 5010 E. FALCON DRIVE SUITE 201 MESA, AZ 85215 | (480)948-4515 |
| CHANDLER AIR SERVICE INC | 1675 E RYAN RD CHANDLER, AZ 85286 | (480)963-6420 |
| COCHISE COMMUNITY COLLEGE DBA: 1. COCHISE COLLEGE | 4190 W HIGHWAY 80, AVIATION DEPT DOUGLAS, AZ 85607 | (520)417-4114 |
| EMBRY-RIDDLE AERONAUTICAL UNIVERSITY - PRESCOTT DBA: 1. EMBRY-RIDDLE AERONAUTICAL UNIVERSITY | 6470 CORRADI WAY PRESCOTT, AZ 86301-3720 | (928)777-4358 |
| EXECUTIVE AVIATION LLC DBA: 1. ARIZONA FLIGHT TRAINING CENTER | 6801 N. GLEN HARBOR BLVD. STE. 107 C GLENDALE, AZ 85307 | (623)877-9334 |
| FALCON EXECUTIVE AVIATION INC | 4766 E. FALCON DRIVE MESA, AZ 85215 | (480)832-0704 |
| GOLD COAST HELICOPTERS | 6801 N. GLEN HARBOR BLVD SUITE 200 GLENDALE, AZ 85307 | (623)935-3388 |
| GUIDANCE ACADEMY LLC DBA: 1. GUIDANCE AVIATION | 6565 CRYSTAL LANE PRESCOTT, AZ 86301 | (928)443-9370 |
| JDO SCHOOL OF AEROSPACE SCIENCES - PHOENIX | UND AEROSPACE FLIGHT TRAINING CTR 5733 SOUTH SOSSAMAN | (480)988-8117 |

RD.
MESA, AZ 85212

| | | |
|---|---|---|
| K AND S AVIATION SERVICES INC | K AND S AVIATION<br>4835 E INDIGO ST.<br>MESA, AZ 85205 | (602)398-1260 |
| K AND S AVIATION SERVICES INC | 4835 E INDIGO STREET<br>SUITE 103<br>MESA, AZ 85205 | (480)398-1260 |
| MPD INC<br>DBA:<br>1. MESA PILOT DEVELOPMENT | 7442 E TILLMAN AVE<br>MESA, AZ 85212 | (480)727-1894 |
| NEW MEXICO FLYING EAGLE INC | 6971 SOUTH APRON<br>DRIVE<br>TUCSON, AZ 85706 | (520)294-1551 |
| NORTH-AIRE INC | 6543 CRYSTAL LANE<br>PRESCOTT, AZ 86301 | (928)445-8320 |
| OXFORD AIRLINE TRAINING<br>CENTER INC<br>DBA:<br>1. OXFORD AVIATION ACADEMY | 1658 S. LITCHFIELD RD.<br>BLD 104<br>STE. 2<br>GOODYEAR, AZ 85338 | (623)882-3466 |
| PHOENIX HELICOPTER SERVICES<br>AZ LLC | TANGO ONE AVIATION<br>4610 E. FIGHTER ACES<br>DR.<br>MESA, AZ 85215 | (480)654-8984 |
| QUANTUM HELICOPTERS INC | 2401 SOUTH HELIPORT<br>WAY<br>CHANDLER, AZ 85286 | (480)814-8118 |
| SONORAN WINGS FLIGHT<br>TRAINING CENTRE INC | 6720 S PLUMER AVE<br>TUCSON, AZ 85756 | (520)807-5900 |
| TIFFIN AVIATION SERVICES INC | HC2 BOX 197-11 ACCESS<br>WAY | (520)287-9120 |

| NOGALES, AZ 85621 | | |
|---|---|---|
| UHI INC | 14700 NORTH AIRPORT DRIVE SUITE 100 SCOTTSDALE, AZ 85262 | (801)377-0077 |
| UHI INC | 2181 SWEGINNIS LOOP SUITE 200 PRESCOTT, AZ 86301 | (928)776-0665 |
| WESTWIND SCHOOL OF AERONAUTICS PHOENIX L L C | 732 WEST DEER VALLEY ROAD PHOENIX, AZ 85027 | (623)869-6973 |

# Arkansas

| Name | Address | Phone |
|---|---|---|
| CENTRAL FLYING SERVICE INC | 1501 BOND STREET LITTLE ROCK, AR 72202 | (501)975-9330 |
| DEPARTMENT OF AVIATION HENDERSON STATE UNIVERSITY | 1100 HENDERSON STREET BOX 7611 ARKADELPHIA, AR 71999-0001 | (870)246-8945 |
| SKYVENTURE AVIATION OF ARKANSAS INC | 4500 SOUTH SCHOOL AVE, SUITE C FAYETTEVILLE, AR 72701 | (479)521-9400 |

# California

| Name | Address | Phone |
|---|---|---|
| ACCESSIBLE AVIATION INTERNATIONAL INC | 3507 JACK NORTHROP HAWTHORNE, CA 90250-4433 | (310)868-8120 |
| ADVENTURE FLIGHTS INC | 2275 GOETZ RD PERRIS, CA 92370 | (951)678-4334 |
| AERO TECH ACADEMY INC | 1745 SESSUMS DRIVE REDLANDS, CA 92374 | (909)794-4046 |
| AHART AVIATION SERVICES INC | 186 AIRWAY BLVD. LIVERMORE, CA 94550 | (925)449-2142 |
| AMERICAN AIRPLANE EXCHANGE INC DBA: 1. ORANGE COUNTY FLIGHT CENTER | 19531 CAMPUS DRIVE SUITE 4 SANTA ANA, CA 92707 | (949)756-1300 |
| AMERICAN AVIATION ACADEMY LLC | 2035 N. MARSHALL AVENUE EL CAJON, CA 92020 | (619)448-9149 |
| AMERICAN FLYERS INC | 2501 AIRPORT AVE SANTA MONICA, CA 90405 | (310)390-2099 |
| AMERICAN HELICOPTERS LLC | 612 W KEARNEY BLVD FRESNO, CA 93706 | (552)233-4411 |
| ANGEL CITY FLYERS INC | 2901-F E SPRING STREET LONG BEACH, CA 90806 | (562)366-4806 |
| ATP PACIFIC INC DBA: 1. BEL-AIR INTERNATIONAL | DBA: BEL-AIR INTERNATIONAL 795 SKY WAY | (650)596-9900 |

| | | |
|---|---|---|
| | SAN CARLOS, CA 94070 | |
| AVIATION FACILITIES INC | 4119 W. COMMONWEALTH AVENUE FULLERTON, CA 92833 | (714)773-0741 |
| AVIATION PACIFIC INC | 16425 VANOWEN STREET VAN NUYS, CA 91406 | (805)612-0931 |
| AVIATOUR INC | 2601 EAST SPRING STREET LONG BEACH, CA 90806 | (562)999-6154 |
| BLUE SKY AVIATION INC DBA: 1. COLLEGE OF THE SEQUOIAS AERONAUTICS & AVIATION TEC | 6627 DALE FRY DR. TULARE, CA 93274 | (559)685-7405 |
| CALIFORINIA AIRWAYS INC | 22693 HESPERIAN BLVD. SUITE 220 HAYWARD, CA 94542 | (510)887-7686 |
| CALIFORNIA AVIATION SERVICES | 6791 AIRPORT DRIVE, SUITE A RIVERSIDE, CA 92504 | (951)354-5274 |
| CALIFORNIA FLIGHT ACADEMY | 2065 NORTH MARSHALL EL CAJON, CA 92020 | (619)448-2212 |
| CALIFORNIA IN NICE INC DBA: 1. NICE AIR | 2575 ROBERT FOWLER WAY SAN JOSE, CA 95148 | (408)729-3383 |
| CANDACE A LARNED ENTERPRISES INC DBA: 1. LONG BEACH FLIGHT ACADEMY | 2631 E. SPRING STREET LONG BEACH, CA 90806 | (562)290-0321 |

| | | |
|---|---|---|
| CHANNEL ISLANDS AVIATION INC | 305 DURLEY AVENUE CAMARILLO, CA 93010 | (805)987-1301 |
| CIVIC HELICOPTERS INC | 2206-H PALOMAR AIRPORT ROAD CARLSBAD, CA 92011 | (760)438-8424 |
| COAST FLIGHT TRAINING AND MANAGEMENT INC | 3753 JOHN J. MONTGOMERY DR. SAN DIEGO, CA 92123 | (858)279-4359 |
| CUTTING EDGE AVIATION INC DBA: 1. CUTTING EDGE HELICOPTERS | 3028 PEACEKEEPER WAY MCCLELLAN, CA 95652 | (916)760-8404 |
| EDWARDS AFB AERO CLUB DBA: 1. EDWARDS AERO CLUB FLIGHT TRAINING CENTER | 5 SELLER AVE. BUILD. 3000 EDWARDS AFB, CA 93524-6745 | (661)275-2376 |
| ENCORE FLIGHT ACADEMY | 16700 ROSCOE BLVD. VAN NUYS, CA 91406 | (888)359-5869 |
| EXECUTIVE FLYERS INC | 6151 FREEPORT BLVD, SUITE 151 EXECUTIVE AIRPORT SACRAMENTO, CA 95822-3530 | (916)427-1888 |
| GLOBAL AVIATORS ACADEMY INC | 1615 MCKINLEY AVE BUILDING B LA VERNE,, CA 91750 | (909)596-1900 |
| GOLDEN EAGLE ENTERPRISES INC DBA: 1. MAZZEI FLYING SERVICE | 4885 E SHIELDS AVENUE SUITE 201 FRESNO, CA 93726 | (559)251-7501 |
| GROUP 3 AVIATION INC | 16425 HART STREET | (818)994-9376 |

| | VAN NUYS, CA 91406 | |
|---|---|---|
| HELIPRO INC | HELIPRO, INC 945B AIRPORT DRIVE SAN LUIS OBISPO, CA 93401 | (805)543-2713 |
| HELISTREAM INC | 3000 AIRWAY AVENUE SUITE 350 COSTA MESA, CA 92626 | (714)662-3163 |
| IASCO FLIGHT CREW TRAINING DIVISION DBA: 1. IASCO FLIGHT TRAINING CENTER | 6460 LOCKHEED DRIVE REDDING, CA 96002 | (530)722-9419 |
| INTERNATIONAL FLIGHT TRAINING ACADEMY INC DBA: 1. IFTA | 1450 BOUGHTON DRIVE BAKERSFIELD, CA 93308 | (661)391-1100 |
| JC AIR ACADEMY INC | 6364 S. LINDBERGH ST. STOCKTON, CA 95206 | (209)983-2773 |
| JEAN'S FLIGHT TRAINING | 1900 JOE CROSSON DR. EL CAJON, CA 92020 | (619)562-1075 |
| K S AVIATION INC DBA: 1. SIERRA ACADEMY OF AERONAUTICS - INTERNT'L TRNG CTR | 2305 JETLIFT DRIVE ATWATER, CA 95301 | (209)722-7522 |
| LOS ANGELES HELICOPTERS LLC | 3501 LAKEWOOD BLVD. LONG BEACH, CA 90808 | (562)377-0396 |
| M I AIR CORPORATION | 1961 AIRPORT DR, UNIT 203 | (424)288-9185 |

| | CORONA, CA 92880 | |
|---|---|---|
| MIRAMAR COLLEGE | 10440 BLACK MOUNTAIN ROAD SAN DIEGO, CA 92126 | (619)358-7664 |
| NATIONAL AIR COLLEGE INC | 3760 GLENN CURTISS ROAD SAN DIEGO, CA 92123 | (858)279-4595 |
| PACIFIC STATES AVIATION INC | 51 JOHN GELNN DRIVE CONCORD, CA 94520 | (925)685-4400 |
| PACIFIC UNION COLLEGE FLIGHT CENTER | ONE ANGWIN AVE PUC FLIGHT CENTER ANGWIN, CA 94508 | (707)965-6219 |
| PINNACLE AVIATION ACADEMY INC | 2210 PALOMAR AIRPORT ROAD CARLSBAD, CA 92011 | (760)929-1009 |
| RISON AVIATION | 1977 NORTH MARSHALL #102 EL CAJON, CA 92020 | (619)258-7247 |
| SAN BERNARDINO VALLEY COLLEGE | 701 S MT VERNON AVE SAN BERNARDINO, CA 92410 | (909)384-8270 |
| SAN DIEGO CHRISTIAN COLLEGE | 2100 GREENFIELD.DRIVE EL CAJON, CA 92109 | (619)590-2171 |
| SAN DIEGO FLIGHT TRAINING INTERNATIONAL INC | 8745 AERO DRIVE, SUITE 103 SAN DIEGO, CA 92123 | (858)569-1822 |
| SCANDINAVIAN AVIATION ACADEMY INC | 1835 N. MARSHALL AVE. EL CAJON, CA 92020 | (619)631-0323 |

| | | |
|---|---|---|
| SHIER AVIATION CORPORATION | 3753 JOHN J. MONTGOMERY DRIVE SUITE 2 SAN DIEGO, CA 92123 | (858)505-5650 |
| SKY WALK INC | 6151 FREEPORT BLVD SUITE 158 SACRAMENTO, CA 95822 | (916)391-1957 |
| SKYWORKS AVIATION INC DBA: 1. TRADEWINDS AVIATION | 2505 CUNNINGHAM AVENUE SAN JOSE, CA 95148 | (408)729-5100 |
| SQUADRON ACQUISITION CORPORATION DBA: 1. SQUADRON 2 | 2655 ROBERT FOWLER WAY SAN JOSE, CA 95148 | (408)272-0518 |
| SUNRISE AVIATION COMPANY INC | 19531 CAMPUS DRIVE SUITE 7 SANTA ANA, CA 92707 | (949)852-8850 |
| THE JETSTREAM GROUP | 7000 MERRILL, B210 SUITE B CHINO, CA 91710 | (909)597-9262 |
| UNIVERSAL AVIATORS ACADEMY INC DBA: 1. UNIVERSAL AIR ACADEMY | 4233 SANTA ANITA AVE. #13 EL MONTE, CA 91731 | (626)454-5254 |
| VOLAR CORPORATION DBA: 1. GOLDEN STATE FLYING SCHOOL | 1640 NORTH JOHNSON AVENUE EL CAJON, CA 92020 | (619)449-0611 |
| WAKITA, YUZO AND IZUMI DBA: 1. AIR ACCORD | 2555 ROBERT FOWLER WAY SAN JOSE, CA 95148 | (408)258-6321 |

| Name | Address | Phone |
|---|---|---|
| WESTERN HELICOPTERS INC | 1640 MIRO WAY UNIT D RIALTO, CA 92377 | (909)829-1056 |
| WINGS FLIGHT SCHOOL | 301 COUNTY AIRPORT ROAD, SUITE 105 VACAVILLE, CA 95688 | (707)449-4647 |

# Colorado

| Name | Address | Phone |
|---|---|---|
| A-CENT AVIATION INC | 1947 AVIATION WAY COLORADO SPRINGS, CO 80916 | (719)573-2236 |
| AIMS COMMUNITY COLLEGE DBA: 1. AIMS COLLEGE FLIGHT TRAINING CENTER | 656 ED BEEGLES LANE BUILDING 56 GREELEY-WELD COUNTY AIRPORT - GREELEY, CO 80631 | (970)356-0790 |
| COLORADO NORTHWESTERN COMMUNITY COLLEGE | 2248 EAST MAIN RANGELY, CO 81648 | (970)675-2261 |
| FLIGHTS INC | 7355 S PEORIA STREET SUITE 111, BOX A16 ENGLEWOOD, CO 80112 | (303)799-5140 |
| FRONT RANGE HELICOPTERS LLC | 4824 EARHART ROAD LOVELAND, CO 80538 | (970)663-7200 |
| JOURNEYS AVIATION | 3335 AIRPORT ROAD, SUITE A BOULDER, CO 80301 | (303)449-4210 |
| MCAIR AVIATION | 11945 AIRPORT WAY BROOMFIELD, CO 80021 | (303)466-8730 |

| METROPOLITAN STATE COLLEGE | METROPOLITAN STATE COLLEGE OF DENVE 1250 7TH ST DENVER, CO 80217-3362 | (303)556-2982 |
| --- | --- | --- |
| ROCKY MOUNTAIN USAF FLIGHT TRAINING CENTER | 325 HAMILTON AVE HANGER 133 PETERSON AFB, CO 80914 | (719)556-4319 |
| ROTORS OF THE ROCKIES INC | 11915 AIRPORT WAY BROOMFIELD, CO 80021 | (303)635-0496 |
| U S A F ACADEMY AERO CLUB | 9222 AIRFIELD DR. PO BOX 77 USAF ACADEMY, CO 808402617 | (719)333-4542 |
| WESTERN AIR FLIGHT ACADEMY | 11915 AIRPORT WAY JEFFERSON COUNTY AIRPORT BROOMFIELD, CO 80021 | (303)466-6998 |

# Connecticut

| Name | Address | Phone |
| --- | --- | --- |
| CONNECTICUT FLIGHT ACADEMY LLP | 20 LINDBERGH DRIVE HARTFORD, CT 06114 | (860)722-9667 |
| INTERSTATE AVIATION INC | 62 JOHNSON AVE PLAINVILLE, CT 06062 | (860)747-5519 |
| KAMAN AEROSPACE CORPORATION | 1332 BLUE HILLS AVE. BLOOMFIELD, CT 06002-0002 | (860)243-7813 |

| NORTHEAST HELICOPTERS FLIGHT SERVICES LLC DBA: 1. NORTHEAST HELICOPTERS | ROUTE 83 HANGER TWO ELLINGTON, CT 06029 | (860)871-2054 |
|---|---|---|
| PREMIER FLIGHT CENTER LLC | 58 LINDBERGH DRIVE HARTFORD, CT 06114 | (860)724-2245 |

# Delaware

| Name | Address | Phone |
|---|---|---|
| DELAWARE STATE UNIVERSITY | AIRWAY SCIENCE DEPT 1200 NORTH DUPONT HIGHWAY DOVER, DE 19901 | (302)857-6710 |
| DOVER AFB AERO CLUB | DOVER AFB AERO CLUB 1360 LAS VEGAS STREET DOVER, DE 19902 | (302)677-6365 |
| HORIZON HELICOPTERS INC | 2035 SUNSET LAKE ROAD NEWARK, DE 19702 | (302)368-5135 |

# Florida

| Name | Address | Phone |
|------|---------|-------|
| 424 AVIATION INC | 13230 SW 132 AVE SUITE 20 MIAMI, FL 33186 | (786)242-4848 |
| ACADEMICS OF FLIGHT | 5000 NW 36TH STREET MIAMI, FL 33266 | (305)870-0862 |
| ADF AIRWAYS DBA: 1. ADF AIRWAYS | RELIANCE BLDG 14532 SW 129 ST MIAMI, FL 33186 | (305)233-6648 |
| AEROSIM FLIGHT ACADEMY | 2700 FLIGHT LINE AVE. SANFORD, FL 32773 | (407)330-7020 |
| AEROSIM FLIGHT ACADEMY | 855-3 ST. JOHNS BLUFF ROAD HANGAR 3 JACKSONVILLE, FL 32225 | (904)641-5774 |
| AEROSIM FLIGHT ACADEMY | BROWARD COMM. COLLEGE,SOUTH CAMPUS BLDG. 99, 7200 PINES BLVD. PEMBROOKE PINES, FL 33024 | (407)330-7020 |
| AIR ORLANDO FLIGHT SCHOOL | 319 N. CRYSTAL LAKE DRIVE ORLANDO, FL 32803 | (407)896-0721 |
| AIRBORNE SYSTEMS INC EURO FLIGHT CONNECTION L C | 2011 S. PERIMETER RD. SUITES G & H FT. LAUDERDALE, FL 33309 | (954)776-0596 |
| AIRCRAFT MANAGEMENT | PETER PRINCE FIELD | (850)623-4151 |

| | | |
|---|---|---|
| SERVICES INC<br>DBA:<br>1. AMS FLIGHT SCHOOL | 5600 NORTH AIRPORT ROAD<br>MILTON, FL 32583 | |
| AIRLINE CAREER ASSOCIATES INC | 4010 4TH ST.<br>301 NORTH DYER BLVD, SUITE 102<br>KISSIMMEE, FL 34741 | (407)518-7766 |
| 1. NIGHT FLIGHT CONCEPTS<br>2. PALM BEACH HELICOPTERS | 2615 LANTANA RD.<br>SUITE A<br>LANTANA, FL 33462 | (561)304-1491 |
| AMERICAN FLIGHT TRAINING LLC | 14351 NW 41 AVE<br>OPA LOCKA, FL 33054 | (305)685-6468 |
| AMERICAN FLYERS INC | 801 N.E. 10TH STREET<br>POMPANO BEACH, FL 33060 | (954)785-1450 |
| ARI BEN AVIATOR INC | 4220 PAN AM BOULEVARD<br>FORT PIERCE, FL 34946 | (772)466-4822 |
| ATP FLIGHT ACADEMY | 1624 AVIATION CENTER PARKWAY<br>DAYTONA BEACH, FL 32114 | (904)273-3018 |
| ATP FLIGHT ACADEMY | 855-602 ST. JOHNS BLUFF ROAD<br>JACKSONVILLE, FL 32225 | (904)641-9281 |
| AVIA FLIGHT ACADEMY INTERNATIONAL INC | 281 OLD MOODY BLVD.<br>PALM COAST, FL 32164 | (386)586-3380 |
| BRISTOW ACADEMY INC | 365 GOLDEN KNIGHTS BLVD<br>TITUSVILLE, FL 32780 | (321)385-2919 |

| | | |
|---|---|---|
| BROWARD COLLEGE | MIRAMAR TOWN CENTER<br>2050 CIVIC COURT PLACE<br>MIRAMAR, FL 33025 | (954)201-8084 |
| BROWARD COLLEGE | 7200 PINES BLVD, BLDG 99<br>AVIATION INSTITUTE<br>PEMBROKE PINES, FL 33024 | (954)201-8084 |
| CAMS FLIGHT INC<br>DBA:<br>1. CAM'S FLIGHT, INC. | 14421 AIRPORT PARKWAY<br>CLEARWATER, FL 33762 | (727)507-8881 |
| CECIL CENTER SOUTH | 13450 LAKE FRETWELL ST.<br>JACKSONVILLE, FL 32211 | (904)634-0315 |
| CIRRUS AVIATION INC | 8191 NORTH TAMIAMI TRAIL<br>SARASOTA, FL 34243 | (941)360-9074 |
| CLEARWATER AVIATION ACADEMY | 14695 AIRPORT PARKWAY<br>CLEARWATER, FL 33762 | (727)538-0318 |
| CLOUD 9 HELICOPTERS LLC | 11610 AVIATION BLVD.<br>SUITE B2<br>WEST PALM BEACH, FL 33412 | (561)799-3636 |
| CLOUD DANCER AVIATION AND FLYING CLUB INC | 1400 FLIGHTLINE BLVD<br>SUITE B<br>DELAND, FL 32724 | (386)238-7270 |
| CRYSTAL AERO GROUP INC | PO BOX 2050<br>CRYSTAL RIVER AIRPORT<br>CRYSTAL RIVER, FL 34423 | (352)795-6868 |

| | | |
|---|---|---|
| DEAN INTERNATIONAL INC | 14150 SW 129TH STREET<br>MIAMI, FL 33186 | (305)259-5611 |
| EGLIN AERO CLUB | PO BOX 1588<br>BLDG. 898<br>EGLIN AFB, FL 32542 | (850)882-5148 |
| EMBRY RIDDLE AERONAUTICAL UNIVERSITY<br>DBA:<br>1. EMBRY-RIDDLE AERONAUTICAL UNIVERSITY | 600 S. CLYDE MORRIS BLVD.<br>DAYTONA BEACH, FL 32114 | (386)226-6810 |
| ENDEAVOUR FLIGHT TRAINING INC | 14970 NW 42 AVE<br>SUITE 117<br>OPA LOCKA, FL 33054 | (305)769-2779 |
| EPIC FLIGHT ACADEMY INC | 600 SKYLINE DRIVE<br>NEW SMYRNA BEACH AIRPORT<br>NEW SMYRNA BEACH, FL 32168 | (386)409-5583 |
| F I T AVIATION LLC<br>DBA:<br>1. FIT AVIATION, LLC | 801 HARRY GOODE WAY<br>MELBOURNE, FL 32901-1885 | (321)674-6500 |
| FLIGHTSAFETY ACADEMY OF DIV OF FLIGHTSAFETY INTL I<br>DBA:<br>1. FLIGHT SAFETY ACADEMY | 3530 CHEROKEE DRIVE<br>VERO BEACH MUNICIPAL AIRPORT<br>VERO BEACH, FL 32960 | (772)564-7600 |
| FLORIDA AVIATION CAREER TRAINING INC | 4900 U.S. 1 NORTH<br>SUITE 200<br>ST. AUGUSTINE, FL 32095 | (904)824-9401 |
| FLORIDA FLIGHT TRAINING CENTER INC | 160 EAST AIRPORT ROAD<br>VENICE, FL 34285 | (941)484-3771 |
| FLORIDA FLYERS EUROPEAN US | 4730 CASA COLA WAY,<br>SUITE #100 | (904)209-3505 |

| | | |
|---|---|---|
| FLIGHT SCHOOL INC | ST AUGUSTINE, FL 32095 | |
| GLEIM INTERNET INC | 4201 NW 95TH BLVD<br>GAINESVILLE, FL 32606 | (352)224-1310 |
| GULF ATLANTIC AIRWAYS INC<br>DBA:<br>1. UNIVERSITY AIR CENTER | 4701 NE 40TH TERRACE<br>GAINESVILLE AIRPORT<br>GAINESVILLE, FL 32609 | (352)373-2426 |
| HELICOPTERACADEMY.COM LLC | HOLLYWOOD/NORTH<br>PERRY AIRPORT<br>603 SW 77TH WAY<br>PEMBROKE PINES, FL<br>33024 | (954)525-9747 |
| INTERNATIONAL TRAINING<br>SYSTEMS INC | 1020 NW 62 ST<br>HANGAR 13 2ND FLOOR<br>FT. LAUDERDALE, FL<br>33309 | (954)584-5899 |
| JACOBS FLIGHT SERVICES LLC | 1090 AIRGLADES BLVD<br>CLEWISTON, FL 33440 | (863)983-2499 |
| JAX NAVY FLYING CLUB | NAVAL AIR STATION<br>JACKSONVILLE<br>BUILDING 847A<br>JACKSONVILLE, FL 32212-<br>0127 | (904)777-8549 |
| LONDON HELICOPTERS INC<br>DBA:<br>1. LONDON AVIATION GROUP | 100 AVIATION DRIVE<br>SOUTH<br>NAPLES, FL 34104 | (239)643-4468 |
| LUNSFORD AIR CONSULTING INC | 201 AIRPORT RD<br>SUITE 1<br>PALM COAST, FL 32164 | (386)586-6098 |
| LYNN UNIVERSITY | 3960 AIRPORT RD.<br>BOCA RATON, FL 33431 | (561)237-7323 |

| | | |
|---|---|---|
| MIAMI DADE COLLEGE | 14715 SW 128 STREET<br>MIAMI, FL 33196 | (305)237-5900 |
| NAPLES AIR CENTER INC | 240 AVIATION DRIVE<br>NORTH<br>NAPLES, FL 34104 | (239)643-1717 |
| NATIONAL AVIATION ACADEMY OF<br>MISSISSIPPI INC<br>DBA:<br>1. NATIONAL AVIATION ACADEMY | 6225 ULMERTON ROAD<br>CLEARWATER, FL 33760 | (727)412-8699 |
| NORTH COUNTY FLIGHT TRAINING<br>LLC | 11550 AVIATION BLVD,<br>SUITE #4<br>WEST PALM BEACH, FL<br>33412 | (561)694-9282 |
| NS AVIATION TRAINING AND<br>RENTAL INC | 601 S. W. 77TH WAY<br>SUITE E<br>PEMBROKE PINES, FL<br>33023 | (954)964-1276 |
| OCALA AVIATION SERVICES INC | 1200 SW 60TH AVE<br>OCALA, FL 34474 | (352)861-7484 |
| OCEAN HELICOPTERS INC | 11550 AVIATION BLVD.,<br>SUITE 1<br>WEST PALM BEACH, FL<br>33412 | (561)625-1900 |
| ORIENT FLIGHT SCHOOL | 28790 SW 217TH AVENUE<br>HOMESTEAD, FL 33030 | (727)251-2396 |
| ORMOND BEACH AVIATION INC<br>1. EURO-AMERICAN SCHOOL OF<br>AVIATION | 770 AIRPORT ROAD, #7<br>ORMOND BEACH, FL<br>32174 | (386)673-9862 |
| PALM BEACH FLIGHT TRAINING<br>CORP | 2633 LANTANA ROAD<br>BUILDING 1101<br>LANTANA, FL 33462 | (561)963-8821 |

| | | |
|---|---|---|
| PARAGON FLIGHT TRAINING | 511 DANLEY DRIVE<br>FORT MYERS, FL 33907 | (239)274-3170 |
| PARIS AIR | 3300 AIRPORT WEST<br>DRIVE<br>VERO BEACH, FL 32960 | (772)770-2708 |
| PELICAN FLIGHT TRAINING LLC | 1601 S W 75TH AVE<br>PEMBROKE PINES, FL<br>33023 | (954)966-9750 |
| PENSACOLA AVIATION CENTER<br>LLC | PENSACOLA REGIONAL<br>AIRPORT<br>4145 JERRY L.<br>MAYGARDEN ROAD<br>PENSACOLA, FL 32504 | (850)434-0636 |
| PHOENIX EAST AVIATION INC | 561 PEARL HARBOR DR<br>REGIONAL AIRPORT<br>DAYTONA BEACH, FL<br>32014 | (386)258-0703 |
| PILOT TRAINING CENTER | 14300 SW 129TH STREET<br>SUITE 204<br>MIAMI, FL 33186 | (305)519-5078 |
| PROFFESIONAL FLIGHT TRAINING | 1815 NW 51 PL<br>FT LAUDERDALE, FL<br>33309 | (954)938-3043 |
| SILVER EXPRESS COMPANY | 14569 SW 127 STREET<br>MIAMI, FL 33186 | (305)255-8753 |
| EUROPE-AMERICAN AVIATION | 200 AVIATION DRIVE<br>NORTH SUITE 6<br>NAPLES MUNICPAL<br>AIRPORT<br>NAPLES, FL 34104 | (239)430-9220 |

| | | |
|---|---|---|
| SKYWARRIOR INC | 4345 JERRY L. MAYGARDEN ROAD PENSACOLA, FL 32504 | (850)433-6115 |
| SPACE COAST AVIATION | 900 AIRPORT ROAD MERRITT ISLAND, FL 32952 | (321)453-2222 |
| STERLING FLIGHT TRAINING BY MALONE AIR INC | 855-21 ST. JOHNS BLUFF ROAD JACKSONVILLE, FL 32225 | (904)642-9683 |
| SUNRISE AVIATION INC | 740 AIRPORT ROAD ORMOND BEACH, FL 32174-8755 | (386)677-5724 |
| SUNSTATE AVIATION | 3008 PATRICK STREET KISSIMMEE, FL 34741 | (407)944-3592 |
| TAILWHEELS ETC | 3000 21ST STREET, NW WINTER HAVEN, FL 33881 | (863)327-6880 |
| TOMLINSON AVIATION INC | 92 HANGAR WAY ORMOND BEACH MUNICIPAL AIRPORT ORMOND BEACH, FL 32174 | (386)676-0312 |
| TREASURE COAST FLIGHT TRAINING | 2580 SE AVIATION WAY SUITE 202 STUART, FL 33496 | (772)219-4191 |
| VOYAGER AVIATION INTERNATIONAL LLC | 475 MANOR DRIVE MERRITT ISLAND, FL 32952-3712 | (321)454-3090 |

# Georgia

| Name | Address | Phone |
|---|---|---|

| | | |
|---|---|---|
| AMERICAN AIR FLIGHT TRAINING INC | 2000 AIRPORT ROAD, SUITE 109 ATLANTA, GA 30341 | (770)455-4203 |
| AMERICAN FLYERS INC | 1950 AIRPORT ROAD ATLANTA, GA 30341 | (678)281-0631 |
| BALLOONACY LTD LLC SCHOOL DBA: 1. BALLOONACY LLC SCHOOL OF APPLIED AEROSTATION 2. BALLOONACY, LTD SCHOOL | 125 REDWOOD CIRCLE FAYETTEVILLE, GA 30214 | (770)719-9492 |
| CENTURY CRM LLC | 111 BATTERY WAY PEACHTREE CITY, GA 30269 | (678)463-4797 |
| FALCON AVIATION ACADEMY LLC DBA: 1. FALCON AVIATION ACADEMY | 95 EAST AVIATION WAY NEWNAN, GA 30263 | (770)486-5561 |
| FALCON AVIATION ACADEMY LLC | 1954 AIRPORT ROAD SUITE 150 DEKALB PEACHTREE AIRPORT ATLANTA, GA 30341 | (770)486-5561 |
| FALCON AVIATION ACADEMY LLC | ATHENS BEN EPPS AIRPORT 1040 BEN EPPS DRIVE ATHENS, GA 30605 | (770)486-5561 |
| FALCON AVIATION ACADEMY LLC | 5 FALCON DRIVE PEACHTREE CITY, GA 30269 | (770)486-5561 |
| FULTON AVIATION LLC | 3984 AVIATION CIRCLE SUITE 200 ATLANTA, GA 30336 | (678)472-4365 |
| GEORGIA AVIATION CAMPUS OF | 71 AIRPORT ROAD | (478)374-6980 |

| | |
|---|---|
| MIDDLE GEORGIA COLLEGE | EASTMAN, GA 31023 |
| QUALITY AVIATION INC | 1951 AIRPORT RD,SUITE 100  (770)457-6215<br>DEKALB-PEACHTREE<br>AIRPORT<br>ATLANTA, GA 30341 |
| ROBINS AFB AERO CLUB | 78TH FORCE SUPPORT          (478)926-4867<br>SQUADRON<br>620 9TH STREET<br>ROBINS AFB, GA 31098 |
| SKYS INTERNATIONAL FLIGHT TRAINING LLC | 115 AIRPORT ROAD, SUITE   (770)253-2774<br>4<br>NEWNAN, GA 30263 |
| THE FLIGHT SCHOOL OF GWINNETT INC | 800 AIRPORT ROAD SUITE   (770)513-0000<br>101<br>LAWRENCEVILLE, GA 30046 |

# Hawaii

| Name | Address | Phone |
|---|---|---|
| ABOVE IT ALL INC<br>DBA:<br>1. HAWAII FLIGHT ACADEMY | 73-300 U'U STREET<br>COMMUTER TERMINAL<br>KONA AIRPORT<br>KAILUA-KONA, HI 96740 | (808)329-0018 |
| ABOVE IT ALL INC | GATE 29, HILO<br>INTERNATIONAL AIRPORT<br>HILO, HI 96720 | (808)961-5140 |
| ANDERSON AVIATION INC | 100 KAULELE PLACE<br>HONOLULU, HI 96819 | (808)833-5899 |
| GALVIN FLIGHT SERVICES HAWAII LLC | 91-1259 MIDWAY ROAD,<br>KAPOLEI, HI 96707 | (808)682-6391 |

| | | |
|---|---|---|
| HAWAII PACIFIC AVIATION INC | 3366 WAAPA RD<br>#507<br>LIHUE, HI 96766 | (808)245-4006 |
| HAWAII PACIFIC AVIATION INC | 90 NAKOLO PL<br>SUITE #2<br>HONOLULU, HI 96819 | (808)834-6779 |
| HAWAII PACIFIC AVIATION INC<br>DBA:<br>1. MAUNA LOA HELICOPTERS | 73-310 U'U STREET<br>SOUTH RAMP<br>KAILUA-KONA, HI 96740 | (808)334-0234 |
| MOORE AIR INC | 90 NAKOLO PLACE, SUITE 24<br>HONOLULU, HI 96819 | (808)833-5628 |
| WASHIN AIR INC<br>DBA:<br>WASHIN AIR | 112 NAKOLO PLACE<br>HONOLULU<br>INTERNATIONAL AIRPORT<br>HONOLULU, HI 96819 | (808)836-3539 |

# Idaho

| Name | Address | Phone |
|---|---|---|
| AVIATION SPECIALTIES UNLIMITED INC | 4632 AERONCA STREET<br>BOISE, ID 83705 | (208)426-8117 |
| JETSTREAM AVIATION INC | 3653 RICKENBACKER<br>BOISE, ID 83705 | (208)345-3730 |
| NORTHERN AIR INC | 64602 HWY 2<br>BONNERS FERRY, ID 83805 | (208)267-4359 |
| PONDEROSA AERO CLUB | 3591 RICKENBACKER STREET | (208)344-5401 |

| | BOISE, ID 83705 | |
|---|---|---|
| SILVERHAWK AVIATION ACADEMY LLC | 4505 AVIATION WAY CALDWELL, ID 83605 | (208)453-8577 |
| UTAH HELICOPTER INC | 1503A FLIGHT LINE DRIVE ALSO MAILING ADDRESS FOR PIH POCATELLO, ID 83204 | (208)233-4365 |
| UTAH HELICOPTER INC | 2381 FOOTE DRIVE ALSO MAILING ADDRESS FOR IDA IDAHO FALLS, ID 83402 | (208)227-0300 |

# Illinois

| Name | Address | Phone |
|---|---|---|
| AIRGO INC | 2331 E CALUMET CENTRALIA, IL 62801 | (618)533-1643 |
| AMERICAN FLYERS INC | 3N040 POWIS RD DUPAGE AIRPORT WEST CHICAGO, IL 60185-1056 | (630)584-4700 |
| BOARD OF TRUSTEES OF SOUTHERN ILLINOIS DBA: 1. ASA AVIATION FLIGHT | SOUTHERN ILLINOIS ARPT CARBONDALE, IL 62901 | (618)453-1147 |
| FLY AMERICA INC | 3232 PLEASANT STREET DEKALB, IL 60115 | (815)751-0917 |
| GREAT RIVER AVIATION LLC | 1647 HIGHWAY 104 QUINCY MUNICIPAL AIRPORT | (217)885-3353 |

| | QUINCY, IL 62305 | |
|---|---|---|
| JA FLIGHT TRAINING | AURORA MUNICIPAL AIRPORT 43W700 US ROUTE 30 SUGAR GROVE, IL 60554 | (630)549-2152 |
| LEWIS UNIVERSITY DBA: 1. LEWIS FLIGHT | ONE UNIVERSITY PARKWAY ROMEOVILLE, IL 60446 | (815)838-0500 |
| MCCLELLAND AVIATION COMPANY INC | 1100 AVIATION LANE SPRINGFIELD, IL 62707 | (217)544-9027 |
| PICME AVIATION | 2001 CAPITAL AIRPORT ABRAHAM LINCOLN CAPITAL AIRPORT SPRINGFIELD, IL 62707 | (217)528-1128 |
| ROTORS AND WINGS AVIATION LLC | 809 E. 4000 SOUTH ROAD KANKAKEE, IL 60901 | (815)939-3575 |
| SCOTT AIR FORCE BASE AERO CLUB | FLIGHT TRAINING CENTER 215 HERITAGE DR. SCOTT AFB, IL 62225 | (618)256-2170 |
| SKILL AVIATION INC | 2346 W. BEACH ROAD WAUKEGAN, IL 60087 | (847)599-9955 |
| SOUTHWESTERN ILLINOIS COLLEGE | SOUTHWESTERN ILLINOIS COLLEGE AVIATION PILOT TRAINING BELLEVILLE, IL 62221 | (618)235-2700 |
| UNIVERSITY OF ILLINOIS | UNIV OF IL WILLARD ARPT | (217)244-8606 |

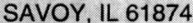

SAVOY, IL 61874

# Indiana

| Name | Address | Phone |
|------|---------|-------|
| GRIFFITH AVIATION INC | 1705 EAST MAIN STREET GRIFFITH, IN 46319 | (219)924-0207 |
| INDY JET HOLDINGS LLC DBA: 1. INDY FLIGHT TRAINING | 3867 AVIATION WAY GREENFIELD, IN 46140 | (317)336-3610 |
| J S AVIATION INC | 1300 ACADEMY ROAD NAVAL BUILDING CULVER, IN 46511 | (219)464-0132 |
| J S AVIATION INC | STARK COUNTY AIRPORT 1793 N 200 EAST KNOX, IN 46534 | (219)464-0132 |
| J S AVIATION INC DBA: 1. EAGLE AIRCRAFT | 4001 MURVIHILL ROAD VALPARAISO, IN 46383 | (219)464-0132 |
| NEW HORIZONS AVIATION INC | 17229 CR 42 GOSHEN, IN 46526 | (574)971-4221 |

# Iowa

| Name | Address | Phone |
|------|---------|-------|

| ADVANCED AIR INC | 16801 MCCANDLESS LN COUNCIL BLUFFS, IA 51442 | (712)323-2173 |
| CARVER AERO INC | 9230 NORTH HARRISON ST DAVENPORT, IA 52806 | (563)391-5650 |
| EXEC1 AVIATION INC | 3700 SE CONVENIENCE BLVD ANKENY, IA 50021 | (515)965-1020 |
| INDIAN HILLS COMMUNITY COLLEGE | AVIATION PROGRAMS 14383 COLLEGE AVENUE OTTUMWA, IA 52501 | (641)683-5214 |
| IOWA COPTER LLC DBA: 1. IOWA HELICOPTER | 3737 SE CONVENIENCE BLVD. ANKENY, IA 50021 | (515)240-4328 |
| IOWA LAKES COMMUNITY COLLEGE | 300 S 18TH ST ESTHERVILLE, IA 51334 | (712)362-2604 |
| STORM FLYING SERVICE INC | 1524 240TH ST MUNI ARPT WEBSTER CITY, IA 50595 | (515)832-3723 |
| UNIVERSITY OF DUBUQUE | 2000 UNIVERSITY AVE DUBUQUE, IA 52001 | (563)589-3834 |

# Kansas

| Name | Address | Phone |
| --- | --- | --- |
| CESSNA EMPLOYEES FLYING CLUB | 1780 AIRPORT ROAD MID-CONTINENT AIRPORT WICHITA, KS 67209 | (316)633-4768 |
| HESSTON COLLEGE AVIATION | PO BOX 3000 | (316)283-6161 |

| | HESSTON, KS 67062-2093 | |
|---|---|---|
| KANSAS STATE UNIVERSITY - SALINA | 2310 CENTENNIAL ROAD SALINA, KS 67401-8058 | (785)826-2679 |
| UHI INC | 2310 CENTENNIAL ROAD SALINA, KS 67401 | (801)377-0077 |
| UHI INC | 102 AIRPORT ROAD DODGE CITY, KS 67801 | (620)225-4054 |

# Kentucky

| Name | Address | Phone |
|---|---|---|
| AERO-TECH INC | 4330 HANGAR DRIVE LEXINGTON, KY 40510 | (859)254-8906 |
| AIR CENTER 1 LLC | 2815 TAYLORSVILLE RD SUITE 105 LOUISVILLE, KY 40205 | (502)451-6451 |
| EASTERN KENTUCKY UNIVERSITY | EASTERN KENTUCKY UNIVERSITY WHALIN TECHNOLOGY COMPLEX, ROOM 307 RICHMOND, KY 40475-3102 | (859)622-1014 |
| NEXGEN AVIATION LLC | 4144 AVIATOR RD SUITE 100 LEXINGTON, KY 40510 | (859)539-3172 |
| THE ACADEMY AT SHAWNEE | 4018 W. MARKET STREET LOUISVILLE, KY 40212 | (502)485-8326 |

# Louisiana

| Name | Address | Phone |
|------|---------|-------|
| BRISTOW ACADEMY INC | 1113 VORTEX DR<br>NEW IBERIA, LA 70560 | (337)364-8909 |
| FLIGHT ACADEMY OF NEW ORLEANS LLC | 502 AIRPORT RD<br>NATCHITOCHES REGIONAL AIRPORT<br>NATCHITOCHES, LA 71457 | (318)354-1444 |
| FLIGHT ACADEMY OF NEW ORLEANS LLC | 6101 GIUSEPPE BELLANCA ST.<br>SUITE 200<br>NEW ORLEANS, LA 70126 | (504)241-9131 |
| FLY-BY-KNIGHT INC | 800 JUDGE LEON FORD DRIVE<br>HAMMOND, LA 70401 | (985)340-8800 |
| GULF COAST AVIATION LLC | LAKEFRONT AIRPORT<br>6401 STARS AND STRIPES BLVD<br>NEW ORLEANS, LA 70126 | (504)246-2700 |
| JPS AVIATION LLC | 5410 OPERATIONS ROAD<br>MONROE, LA 71203 | (318)387-0222 |
| LOUISIANA TECH UNIVERSITY | 136 AVIATION BLVD<br>RUSTON REGIONAL AIRPORT<br>RUSTON, LA 71272 | (318)257-2691 |
| SOUTHERN SEAPLANE INC | 1 COQUILLE DR.<br>BELLE CHASSE, LA 70037 | (504)394-6959 |

# Maine

| Name | Address | Phone |
|------|---------|-------|

| | | |
|---|---|---|
| AIRLINK LLC | 2 LAFLEUR ROAD WATERVILLE, ME 04901 | (207)859-0109 |
| MAINE COASTAL FLIGHT CENTER INC | 112 CARUSO DRIVE TRENTON, ME 04605 | (207)664-6000 |
| MAINE INSTRUMENT FLIGHT | 215 WINTHROP STREET AUGUSTA STATE AIRPORT AUGUSTA, ME 04330 | (207)622-1211 |
| SOUTHERN MAINE AVIATION LLC | 199 AIRPORT ROAD SANFORD REGIONAL AIRPORT SANFORD, ME 04073 | (207)324-8919 |

# Maryland

| Name | Address | Phone |
|---|---|---|
| BRETT AVIATION INC | MARTIN STATE AIRPORT 701 WILSON POINT ROAD MIDDLE RIVER, MD 21220 | (410)391-0210 |
| FREDERICK FLIGHT CENTER INC | 330 AVIATION WAY FREDERICK MUNICIPAL AIRPORT FREDERICK, MD 21701 | (240)529-5500 |
| FREEWAY AIRPORT INC | 3900 CHURCH ROAD MITCHELLVILLE, MD 20721 | (301)390-6424 |
| GT AVIATION INC | 10300 GLEN WAY FT. WASHINGTON, MD, MD 20744 | (301)241-1711 |
| NAVY ANNAPOLIS FLIGHT CENTER | 3090 SOLOMONS ISLAND RD HANGAR D | (410)956-8751 |

| DBA:<br>1. NAVY ANNAPOLIS FLIGHT<br>CENTER | EDGEWATER, MD 21037-1402 | |
| TRIDENT AVIATION | BAY BRIDGE AIRPORT<br>206 AIRPORT ROAD<br>STEVENSVILLE, MD 21666 | (410)604-1333 |

# Massachusetts

| Name | Address | Phone |
| --- | --- | --- |
| BLUE HILL HELICOPTERS INC | 125 ACCESS ROAD<br>NORWOOD, MA 02062 | (781)688-0263 |
| BRIDGEWATER STATE UNIVERSITY | 111 HARINGTON HALL<br>95 GROVE STREET<br>BRIDGEWATER, MA 02325 | (508)717-8726 |
| BRIDGEWATER STATE UNIVERSITY | NEW BEDFORD REGIONAL AIRPORT<br>1852 SHAWMUT AVE<br>NORTH DARTMOUTH, MA 02747 | (508)531-1445 |
| EAST COAST AERO CLUB | 106 ACCESS ROAD<br>NORWORD MEMORIAL AIRPORT<br>NORWOOD, MA 02062 | (781)278-8800 |
| EXECUTIVE FLYERS AVIATION INC | 492 SUTTON STREET<br>HANGAR 89<br>NORTH ANDOVER, MA 01846 | (781)274-7477 |
| EXECUTIVE FLYERS AVIATION INC<br>DBA:<br>1. EXECUTIVE FLYERS | EXECUTIVE FLYERS AVIATION CORP.<br>HANSCOM FIELD | (781)274-7227 |

| AVIATION CORPORATION | BEDFORD, MA 01730 | |
|---|---|---|
| FIVE STAR FLIGHT ACADEMY | WESTFIELD STATE COLLEGE 577 WESTERN AVENUE WESTFIELD, MA 01086-1630 | (413)572-5590 |
| FIVE STAR FLIGHT ACADEMY DBA: 1. WESTFIELD FLIGHT ACADEMY | BARNES-WESTFIELD AIRPORT 11 AIRPORT ROAD WESTFIELD, MA 01085 | (413)568-5800 |
| HANSCOM FLIGHT TRAINING CENTER | 7 ROBBINS ROAD BLDG 1722 HANSCOM AFB, MA 01731 | (781)377-5160 |
| NATIONAL AVIATION ACADEMY OF NEW ENGLAND | 150 HANSCOM DRIVE HANSCOM AIRPORT BEDFORD, MA 01730 | (781)274-8445 |
| NORTH ANDOVER FLIGHT ACADEMY | LAWRENCE AIRPORT 492 SUTTON STREET NORTH ANDOVER, MA 01845 | (978)689-7600 |
| NORTH SHORE COMMUNITY COLLEGE | 1 FERNCROFT ROAD ROOM 366M DANVERS, MA 01923 | (978)739-5592 |
| NORTHAMPTON AERONAUTICS INC | 160 OLD FERRY ROAD NORTHAMPTON, MA 01060 | (413)584-7980 |

# Michigan

| Name | Address | Phone |
|---|---|---|

| | | |
|---|---|---|
| AMERICAN WINGS AVIATION LLC | 3375 W. BRISTOL RD BISHOP IAP FLINT, MI 48507 | (810)233-6448 |
| EXECUTIVE AIR TRANSPORT INC | 103 SINCLAIR DRIVE MUSKEGON, MI 49441 | (231)798-2126 |
| NORTHWESTERN MICHIGAN COLLEGE | 2600 AERO PARK DRIVE TRAVERSE CITY, MI 49686 | (231)995-1220 |
| SOLO AVIATION INC | 801 AIRPORT DR ANN ARBOR, MI 48108 | (734)994-6651 |
| TRUMBULL AVIATION LLC DBA: 1. EAGLE FLIGHT CENTRE | 830 WILLOW RUN AIRPORT YPSILANTI, MI 48198 | (734)481-3000 |
| WESTERN MICHIGAN UNIVERSITY COLLEGE OF AVIATION | 237 NORTH HELMER ROAD BATTLE CREEK, MI 49037 | (269)964-4029 |

# Minnesota

| Name | Address | Phone |
|---|---|---|
| ACADEMY COLLEGE | 1101 E. 78TH STREET SUITE 100 BLOOMINGTON, MN 55420 | (952)851-0066 |
| HUMMINGBIRD VENTURES LLC DBA: 1. HUMMINGBIRD AVIATION, LLC 2. HUMMINGBIRD HELICOPTERS OF | 13601 PIONEER TRAIL EDEN PRAIRIE, MN 55347 | (952)944-2628 |

MINNESOTA, LLC

| | | |
|---|---|---|
| JDO SCHOOL OF AEROSPACE SCIENCES - CROOKSTON | CROOKSTON MUNICIPAL AIRPORT CROOKSTON, MN 56716 | (218)281-1690 |
| LAKE SUPERIOR HELICOPTERS LLC | 210 WEST MICHIGAN STREET SUITE 300 DULUTH, MN 55802 | (866)566-1940 |
| MN AVIATION INC | PO BOX 369 400 AIRPORT ROAD ALBERT LEA, MN 56007 | (507)373-9265 |
| MN HELICOPTERS INC | 8891AIRPORT ROAD NE E13 BLAINE, MN 55449 | (763)780-2898 |
| NORTH STAR AVIATION INC | 3030 AIRPORT ROAD NORTH MANKATO, MN 56001 | (507)626-6006 |
| ST CLOUD STATE UNIVERSITY | DEPT OF AVIATION HEADLEY HALL HH-216 ST CLOUD, MN 56301 | (320)255-2108 |
| THUNDERBIRD AVIATION INC | 1101 E. 78TH STREET SUITE 100 BLOOMINGTON, MN 55420 | (952)851-0066 |
| THUNDERBIRD AVIATION INC | 5800 CRYSTAL AIRPORT ROAD CRYSTAL, MN 55429 | (763)533-4162 |
| THUNDERBIRD AVIATION INC | 14091 PIONEER TRAIL EDEN PRAIRIE, MN 55343 | (952)941-1212 |
| TWIN CITIES FLIGHT TRAINING INC | 8891 AIRPORT ROAD HANGAR ROW 2141 RHODE ISLAND BLAINE, MN 55449 | (763)780-4375 |

| VALTERS AVIATION SERVICE STATION INC DBA: 1. VALTERS AVIATION, INC | 3275 MANNING AVENUE NORTH LAKE ELMO, MN 55042 | (651)777-1399 |
| --- | --- | --- |

# Mississippi

| Name | Address | Phone |
| --- | --- | --- |
| ACCESSIBLE AVIATION INTERNATIONAL INC | 1900 AIRPORT ROAD BDG 1 COLUMBUS, MS 39701 | (662)574-9157 |
| AIR VENTURE FLIGHT CENTER | 11299 AIRPORT ROAD OLIVE BRANCH, MS 38654 | (901)521-1068 |
| DELTA STATE UNIVERSITY | COMMERCIAL AVIATION BUILDING DELTA STATE UNIVERSITY CLEVELAND, MS 38733 | (662)846-6083 |

# Missouri

| Name | Address | Phone |
| --- | --- | --- |
| ATD FLIGHT SYSTEMS LLC | 601 LOU HOLLAND DRIVE KANSAS CITY, MO 64116 | (816)221-8455 |
| CAREER PILOT SCHOOL LLC | MIDWEST NATIONAL AIR CENTER 13106 RHODUS ROAD EXCELSIOR SPRINGS, MO 64024 | (816)407-3390 |
| RLS RENTAL COMPANY DBA: 1. MIZZOU AVIATION | D/B/A MIZZOU AVIATION 5497 DENNIS WEAVER DR JOPLIN, MO 64802 | (417)623-1331 |

| ST CHARLES FLYING SERVICE INC | 6016 PORTAGE ROAD PORTAGE DES SOUIX, MO 63373 | (636)946-6066 |
| --- | --- | --- |
| ST LOUIS UNIVERSITY PARKS COLLEGE OF ENG AND AVIAT | 3450 LINDELL BLVD., ST. LOUIS, MO 63103 | (314)977-8283 |
| UNIVERSITY OF CENTRAL MISSOURI | UCM FLIGHT FACILITY MAX B. SWISHER SKYHAVEN AIRPORT WARRENSBURG, MO 64093 | (660)543-4921 |

# Montana

| Name | Address | Phone |
| --- | --- | --- |
| CANYON LAKE HELICOPTERS LLC | 516 AIRPORT ROAD HAMILTON, MT 59840 | (406)360-6842 |
| HOMESTEAD HELICOPTERS INC | 4 CORPORATE WAY MISSOULA, MT 59808 | (406)721-0402 |
| INTERNATIONAL HELICOPTER TRAINING ACADEMY | 1940 AIRPORT COURT GREAT FALLS, MT 59404 | (406)799-0507 |
| MONTANA AERO INC | 9015 CARTAGE ROAD MISSOULA, MT 59808 | (406)543-4777 |
| NORTHERN SKIES AVIATION INC | 3900 FOX ROAD (UPS & FED EX) LAUREL AIRPORT LAUREL, MT 59044 | (406)628-2219 |
| PRAIRIE AVIATION INC | 516 AIRPORT ROAD HAMILTON, MT 59840 | (406)363-6471 |
| RED EAGLE AVIATION INC | 1880 HIGHWAY 93 SOUTH KALISPELL, MT 59901 | (406)755-2376 |

| ROCKY MOUNTAIN COLLEGE | 1511 POLY DRIVE BILLINGS, MT 59102 | (406)254-9525 |
|---|---|---|
| ROCKY MOUNTAIN ROTORS LLC | 305 AVIATION LANE BELGRADE, MT 59714 | (406)579-9312 |
| SUMMIT AVIATION INC | 490 GALLATIN FIELD ROAD BELGRADE, MT 59714 | (406)388-8359 |

# Nebraska

| Name | Address | Phone |
|---|---|---|
| LEMAY FLIGHT TRAINING CENTER | P O BOX 13234 HANGAR 1, BLDG 306 OFFUTT AFB, NE 68113 | (402)294-3385 |
| UNIVERSITY OF NEBRASKA AT KEARNEY | 905 W 25TH ST KEARNEY, NE 68849 | (308)865-8309 |

# Nevada

| Name | Address | Phone |
|---|---|---|
| CACTUS AVIATION | 3500 EXECUTIVE TERMINAL SUITE 250 HENDERSON, NV 89052 | (702)261-4883 |
| ELITE AVIATION VGT LLC DBA: 1. ELITE AVIATION 2. ELITE FLIGHT TRAINING AND MANAGEMENT | 2634 AIRPORT DRIVE, SUITE 103 NORTH LAS VEGAS, NV 89032 | (702)835-1222 |

| MONARCH SKY LLC | 1420 JET STREAM DRIVE SUITE 105 HENDERSON, NV 89052 | (702)631-0386 |

# New Hampshire

| Name | Address | Phone |
| --- | --- | --- |
| AIR DIRECT AIRWAYS DBA: 1. AIR DIRECT AIRWAYS FLIGHT ACADEMY | 125 PERIMETER ROAD NASHUA, NH 03063 | (603)882-5606 |
| DANIEL WEBSTER COLLEGE INC | 20 UNIVERSITY DRIVE NASHUA, NH 03063-1300 | (603)577-6570 |

# New Jersey

| Name | Address | Phone |
| --- | --- | --- |
| AERO SAFETY TRAINING LTD | 425 BEAVERBROOK ROAD LINCOLN PARK, NJ 07035 | (973)872-6213 |
| AIR FLEET TRAINING SYSTEMS INC | ESSEX COUNTY AIRPORT 35 WRIGHT WAY FAIRFIELD, NJ 07004 | (973)575-8220 |
| AMERICAN FLYERS INC | 50 AIRPORT ROAD SUITE 120 MORRISTOWN, NJ 07960 | (973)267-3223 |
| CAVE FLIGHT SCHOOL LLC DBA: 1. AERO PREP INSTITUTE | 60 FOSTERTOWN ROAD MEDFORD, NJ 08055 | (609)267-7673 |
| CENTURY AIR INC | 19 WRIGHT WAY ESSEX COUNTY AIRPORT | (973)575-4800 |

| | FAIRFIELD, NJ 07004 | |
|---|---|---|
| EAGLES ARIE LLC | SUSSEX AIRPORT<br>55 COUNTY ROAD 639<br>SUSSEX, NJ 07461 | (973)600-6333 |
| HERLIHY HELICOPTERS INC<br>DBA:<br>1. HELICOPTER FLIGHT<br>SERVICES | FLYING W AIRPORT<br>60 FOSTERTOWN ROAD<br>MEDFORD, NJ 08055 | (609)265-0822 |
| MERCER COUNTY COMMUNITY<br>COLLEGE | 1200 OLD TRENTON RD<br>MERCER COUNTY<br>COMMUNITY COLLEGE<br>WEST WINDSOR, NJ 08550-<br>3407 | (609)883-0555 |
| MONMOUTH AIRCRAFT<br>SERVICE INC<br>DBA:<br>1. OCEAN AIRE | R.J. MILLER AIRPARK<br>POST OFFICE BOX 1245<br>TOMS RIVER, NJ 08754 | (732)797-1077 |
| PRIVILEGE AERO LLC | 1034 MILLSTONE RIVER<br>ROAD<br>HILLSBOROUGH, NJ 08844 | (908)346-3875 |
| PRIVILEGE AERO LLC | 1034 MILLSTONE RIVER<br>ROAD<br>HILLSBOROUGH, NJ 08844 | (908)346-3875 |
| SKY TRAINING LLC | 126 AIRPORT ROAD<br>WEST MILFORD, NJ 07480 | (973)728-7721 |

# New Mexico

| Name | Address | Phone |
|---|---|---|
| AIRBORNE HEAT LLC | 5001 CROWNPOINT CT. NW<br>ALBUQUERQUE, NM 87120 | (505)604-2865 |

| | | |
|---|---|---|
| BLUE FEATHER AERO FLIGHT SCHOOL | BLUE FEATHER AERO DONA ANNA COUNTY AIRPORT SANTA TERESA, NM 88008 | (575)589-4586 |
| BODE AVIATION INC | 2505 CLARK CARR LOOP, SE ALBUQUERQUE, NM 87106 | (505)884-4530 |
| BODE AVIATION INC | 7401 PASEO DEL VOLCAN, N.W. ALBUQUERQUE, NM 87121 | (505)884-4530 |
| HOLLOMAN AFB AERO CLUB | 420 DELAWARE AVENUE BLDG #283 HOLLOMAN AFB, NM 88330 | (575)572-3752 |
| KIRTLAND FLIGHT CENTER | 3400 CLARK AVE ALBUQUERQUE, NM 87117-5000 | (505)846-1072 |
| NEW MEXICO RADIO SALES DBA: 1. THE BALLOON FLIGHT SCHOOL | 1220 ROCKROSE ROAD, NE ALBUQUERQUE, NM 87122 | (505)821-8558 |

# New York

| Name | Address | Phone |
|---|---|---|
| ACADEMICS OF FLIGHT | 46-12 QUEENS BLVD STE204 SUNNYSIDE, QUEENS NEW YORK, NY 11104 | (718)937-5716 |

| | | |
|---|---|---|
| ACADEMY OF AVIATION LLC | 7150 REPUBLIC AIRPORT ROOM 101 FARMINGDALE, NY 11735 | (631)777-7772 |
| DUNKIRK AVIATION SALES AND SERVICE INC DBA: 1. DUNKIRK AVIATION FLIGHT SCHOOL 2. JAMESTOWN AVIATION CO., LLC. | CHAUTAUQUA COUNTY AIRPORT/DUNKIRK 3389 MIDDLE ROAD DUNKIRK, NY 14048 | (716)366-6938 |
| EAST HILL FLYING CLUB INC | TOMPKINS COUNTY ARPT 62 BROWN RD. ITHACA, NY 14850 | (607)351-3637 |
| FARMINGDALE STATE COLLEGE | REPUBLIC AIRPORT 885 BROADHOLLOW ROAD FARMINGDALE, NY 11735 | (631)420-2036 |
| HERITAGE FLIGHT ACADEMY | 2075 SMITHTOWN AVE RONKONKOMA, NY 11779 | (631)471-3550 |
| JAMESTOWN AVIATION COMPANY LLC | 3163 AIRPORT DRIVE BOX 5 JAMESTOWN, NY 14701 | (716)665-4800 |
| PRIOR AVIATION SERVICE INC | BUFFALO NIAGARA INT'L AIRPORT 50 N AIRPORT DRIVE BUFFALO, NY 14225-1490 | (716)633-1000 |
| RICHMOR AVIATION INC | SCHENECTADY COUNTY AIRPORT 19 AIRPORT ROAD SCOTIA, NY 12302 | (518)399-8171 |
| RICHMOR AVIATION INC | 84 CITATION DRIVE WAPPINGERS FALLS, NY | (845)462-2900 |

| 12590 | | |
|---|---|---|
| ROCHESTER AIR CENTER LLC | 1313 SCOTTSVILLE ROAD ROCHESTER, NY 14624 | (585)328-8839 |

# North Carolina

| Name | Address | Phone |
|---|---|---|
| CALDWELL COMMUNITY COLLEGE AND TECHNICAL INSTITUTE | 2855 HICKORY BLVD. HUDSON, NC 28638 | (828)726-2387 |
| CLEAR DAY AVIATION INC DBA: 1. BURLINGTON AVIATION | 3510 ALAMANCE ROAD BURLINGTON, NC 27215 | (336)227-1278 |
| DILLONS AVIATION INC | 1105 NORTH MEMORIAL DRIVE GREENVILLE, NC 27834 | (252)757-1841 |
| GUILFORD TECHNICAL COMMUNITY COLLEGE | T.H. DAVIS AVIATION CENTER 620 N. REGIONAL ROAD GREENSBORO, NC 27409 | (336)454-1126 |
| HELIVISION LLC DBA: 1. HELIVENTURES | CONCORD REGIONAL AIRPORT 9000 AVIATION BLVD. SUITE 219 CONCORD, NC 28027 | (704)792-1807 |
| JACKSONVILLE FLYING SERVICE | 278 ALBERT ELLIS AIRPORT ROAD RICHLANDS, NC 28574 | (910)324-2500 |
| TAA FLIGHT TRAINING LLC | 7680 AIRLINE RD GREENSBORO, NC 27409 | (336)369-2827 |

| TRIAD AIR INC DBA: 1. PIEDMONT FLIGHT TRAINING | 3815 NORTH LIBERTY STREET WINSTON-SALEM, NC 27105 | (336)776-6070 |
| WNC AVIATION LLC | 21 AVIATION WAY FLETCHER, NC 28732 | (828)650-6540 |

# North Dakota

| Name | Address | Phone |
| --- | --- | --- |
| JDO SCHOOL OF AEROSPACE SCIENCES-GRAND FORKS | UNIVERSTIY OF NORTH DAKOTA PO BOX 8216 UNIVERSITY STATION GRAND FORKS, ND 58202-8216 | (701)777-2791 |

# Ohio

| Name | Address | Phone |
| --- | --- | --- |
| AMERICAN WINDS FLIGHT ACADEMY INC | 1600 TRIPLETT BLVD AKRON FULTON INTERNATIONAL AIRPORT AKRON, OH 44306 | (330)733-2500 |
| AMERICAN WINDS FLIGHT ACADEMY INC | 1600 SOUTH ARLINGTON ROAD SUTIE 100 AKRON, OH 44306 | (330)733-2500 |
| AVIATION SALES INC | 10 WEST 3D ST DAYTON, OH 45429 | (937)885-3662 |
| AVIATION SALES INC | DAYTON INTERNATIONAL AIRPORT | |

| | 501 N. DIXIE DR VANDALIA, OH 45377 | (937)885-3662 |
|---|---|---|
| AVIATION SALES INC | 10600 SPRINGBORO PIKE DAYTON-WRIGHT BROS. AIRPORT MIAMISBURG, OH 45342 | (937)885-3662 |
| AVIATORS FLIGHT ACADEMY LLC | 4335 GLENDALE-MILFORD RD CINCINNATI, OH 45242 | (513)984-5880 |
| BOWLING GREEN STATE UNIVERSITY | COLLEGE OF TECHNOLOGY WOOD COUNTY AIRPORT BOWLING GREEN, OH 43403-0301 | (419)372-2870 |
| FLAMINGO AIR ACADEMY | 262 WILMER AVE. CINCINNATI, OH 45226 | (513)321-7465 |
| HIGHER GROUND HELICOPTERS | 1701 RUN WAY MIDDLETOWN, OH 45042 | (513)217-6700 |
| KENT STATE UNIVERSITY DBA: 1. AERONAUTICS DEPARTMENT/ COLLEGE OF TECHNOLOGY | 4020 KENT ROAD STOW, OH 44224-0001 | (330)672-2610 |
| MIDDLETOWN REGIONAL FLIGHT TRAINING INSTITUTE LLC | 1707 RUN WAY MIDDLETOWN, OH 45042 | (513)217-4636 |
| OHIO UNIVERSITY | DEPARTMENT OF AVIATION OHIO UNIVERSITY ALBANY, OH 45710 | (740)597-2626 |
| PREMIER FLIGHT ACADEMY LTD | BURKE LAKEFRONT AIRPORT 1501 NORTH MARGINAL ROAD | (216)333-1537 |

| | CLEVELAND, OH 44114 | |
| --- | --- | --- |
| SPORTYS ACADEMY INC | CLERMONT COUNTY AIRPORT 2001 SPORTY'S DR BATAVIA, OH 45103 | (513)735-9100 |
| STRATUS HELICOPTERS LLC | 654 WILMER AVE CINCINNATI, OH 45226 | (513)533-4354 |
| T AND G FLYING CLUB INC | 1501 NORTH MARGINAL RD. SUITE 184 CLEVELAND, OH 44114 | (216)241-2321 |
| T AND G FLYING CLUB INC | 26300 CRUTISS WRIGHT PKWY. AREA B RICHMOND HTS., OH 44143 | (216)289-5094 |
| THE OHIO STATE UNIVERSITY | 2160 WEST CASE ROAD HANGAR 5 COLUMBUS, OH 43235-2526 | (614)292-5614 |
| V1 AVIATION TRAINING INC | 95 5TH STREET WAYNESVILLE, OH 45068 | (937)725-0813 |
| WRIGHT PATTERSON AFB AERO CLUB | BLDG 153, 5995 SKEEL AVENUE WPAFB, OH 45433 | (937)257-7714 |

# Oklahoma

| Name | Address | Phone |
| --- | --- | --- |
| CRUMPTON AVIATION LLC | 9051 S. AIRPORT WAY TULSA, OK 74132 | (918)209-4900 |

| OKLAHOMA AVIATION LLC | 7200 NW 63RD, SUITE 121 BETHANY, OK 73008 | (405)787-4568 |
| OKLAHOMA STATE UNIVERSITY DBA: 1. O.S.U. FLIGHT CENTER | 1818 WEST WRIGHT DRIVE STILLWATER, OK 74075 | (405)744-2739 |
| RIVERSIDE FLIGHT CENTER INC | 203 CESSNA DRIVE RICHARD LLOYD JONES, JR. AIRPORT TULSA, OK 74132 | (918)298-3164 |
| SOUTHEASTERN OKLA STATE UNIV DEPT OF AEROSPACE | EAKER FIELD DURANT, OK 74701 | (580)745-3252 |
| SPARTAN AVIATION INDUSTRIES INC DBA: 1. SPARTAN COLLEGE OF AERONAUTICS AND TECHNOLOGY | 123 CESSNA DRIVE R.L. JONES AIRPORT TULSA, OK 74132 | (918)836-6886 |
| TULSA COMMUNITY COLLEGE | 801 EAST 91ST STREET TULSA, OK 74132 | (918)828-4254 |
| UNIVERSITY OF OKLAHOMA | DEPARTMENT OF AVIATION 1700 LEXINGTON AVENUE NORMAN, OK 73069 | (405)325-7231 |
| WESTERN OKLAHOMA STATE COLLEGE DBA: 1. WESTERN OKLAHOMA STATE COLLEGE PIONAIR FLYING CLUB | 2801 NORTH MAIN STREET ALTUS AIRPORT ALTUS, OK 73521 | (580)477-7941 |

# Oregon

| Name | Address | Phone |
|---|---|---|
| CIRRUS AVIATION LLC | 4000 CIRRUS AVENUE MCMINNVILLE, OR 97128 | (503)472-0558 |
| ERICKSON AIR-CRANE INCORPORATED | 3100 WILLOW SPRINGS RD CENTRAL POINT, OR 97502 | (541)664-5544 |
| GORGE WINDS AVIATION INC | 920 NW PERIMETER WAY TROUTDALE, OR 97060 | (503)665-2823 |
| HILLSBORO AVIATION INC | 911 NW GRAHAM ROAD TROUTDALE, OR 97060 | (503)489-1142 |
| HILLSBORO AVIATION INC DBA: 1. AIRMANS PROFICIENCY CENTER 2. HILLSBORO HELICOPTERS | 3565 NE CORNELL RD HILLSBORO, OR 97124 | (503)648-2831 |
| HONEY B LLC DBA: CORVALLIS AERO SERVICE | 5695 SW AIRPORT WAY CORVALLIS, OR 97333 | (541)753-4466 |
| LANE COMMUNITY COLLEGE | 28715 AIRPORT RD EUGENE, OR 97402 | (541)463-4195 |
| LEADING EDGE AVIATION INC | 63048 POWELL BUTTE HIGHWAY BEND, OR 97701 | (541)383-8825 |
| PRECISION FLIGHT TRAINING | 17770 NE AVIATION WAY NEWBERG, OR 97132 | (503)537-0108 |

| | | |
|---|---|---|
| THE FLIGHT SHOP INC<br>DBA:<br>1. PROFESSIONAL AIR | 63132 POWELL BUTTE RD<br>BEND, OR 97701 | (541)388-0019 |
| WILLAMETTE AVIATION<br>SERVICES LLC | 23115 AIRPORT ROAD NE<br>#8<br>AURORA, OR 97002 | (503)678-2252 |

# Pennsylvania

| Name | Address | Phone |
|---|---|---|
| ACE PILOT TRAINING | LEHIGH VALLEY INT'L.<br>AIRPORT<br>600 HAYDEN CIRCLE<br>ALLENTOWN, PA 18109 | (610)264-1105 |
| AERO-TECH SERVICES INC | 500 AIRPORT ROAD.<br>SUITE P<br>LITITZ, PA 17543 | (717)394-2675 |
| AVIATION CERTIFICATION<br>AND EDUCATION SOLUTIONS<br>INC<br>DBA:<br>1. ACES AVIATION | BEAVER COUNTY<br>AIRPORT<br>7 PIPER STREET<br>BEAVER FALLS, PA<br>15010 | (724)891-2237 |
| COMMUNITY COLLEGE OF<br>ALLEGHENY COUNTY | SOUTH CAMPUS<br>1750 CLAIRTON ROAD<br>WEST MIFFLIN, PA<br>15122-3097 | (412)469-6222 |
| COMMUNITY COLLEGE OF<br>BEAVER COUNTY | ONE CAMPUS DRIVE<br>MONACA, PA 15061-2588 | (724)775-8561 |
| GATEWAY AVIATION LTD INC | QUEEN CITY AIRPORT<br>1730 VULTEE ST.<br>ALLENTOWN, PA 18103 | (610)797-7942 |

Career Pilot Blueprint

| | | |
|---|---|---|
| HASKI AVIATION INC | 406 FRANK FARONE DRIVE NEW CASTLE MUNICIPAL AIRPORT NEW CASTLE, PA 16101 | (724)652-5546 |
| HORTMAN AVIATION SERVICES INC | NORTHEAST PHILADELPHIA AIRPORT 9800 ASHTON ROAD PHILADELPHIA, PA 19114 | (215)969-0311 |
| LEHIGH CARBON COMMUNITY COLLEGE | 600 HAYDEN CIRCLE AVIATION DEPT., HANGAR 7 ALLENTOWN, PA 18109 | (610)264-7089 |
| MARYWOOD UNIVERSITY | 2300 ADAMS AVENUE WILLIAM G. MCGOWAN CENTER SCRANTON, PA 18509-1598 | (570)348-6211 |
| MOORE AVIATION INC | BEAVER COUNTY AIRPORT SEVEN PIPER STREET BEAVER FALLS, PA 15010 | (724)843-4800 |
| MOYER AVIATION INC | BRADEN AIRPARK 3800 SULLIVAN TRAIL EASTON, PA 18040 | (610)258-0473 |
| MTT AVIATION SERVICES INC | 469 AIRPORT ROAD JOHNSTOWN, PA 15904 | (814)361-3500 |
| STEEL CITY AVIATION DBA: 1. PITTSBURGH FLIGHT TRAINING CENTER | ALLEGHENY COUNTY AIRPORT_____ HANGAR 7 WEST MIFFLIN, PA 15122 | (412)466-1111 |

183

| | | |
|---|---|---|
| TECH AVIATION FLIGHT SCHOOL INC | 101 HANGAR ROAD AVOCA, PA 18641 | (570)414-0223 |
| VALLEY AVIATION FLIGHT SCHOOL | WYOMING VALLEY AIRPORT 2001 WYOMING AVE FORTY FORT, PA 18704 | (570)288-3257 |

## Puerto Rico

| Name | Address | Phone |
|---|---|---|
| ISLA GRANDE FLYING SCHOOL | ISLA GRANDE AIRPORT NORTH RAMP, LOT G-6 SAN JUAN, PR 00907 | (787)722-1160 |

## Rhode Island

| Name | Address | Phone |
|---|---|---|
| NEW HORIZON AVIATION INC | 2500 POST ROAD WARWICK, RI 02886 | (401)736-5115 |
| NEW HORIZON AVIATION INC | T.F. GREEN AIRPORT HANGAR 1 WARWICK, RI 02886 | (401)736-5115 |
| NEW HORIZON AVIATION INC | T.F. GREEN AIRPORT 660 AIRPORT ROAD WARWICK, RI 02886 | (401)736-5115 |

## South Carolina

| Name | Address | Phone |
|---|---|---|
| BOB JONES UNIVERSITY | 10 OPPORTUNITY PLACE GREENVILLE, SC 29607 | (864)987-9330 |

| CHARLESTON AFB AERO CLUB | 101 FIGHTER DRIVE CHARLESTON AFB, SC 29404 | (843)963-5149 |
| --- | --- | --- |
| INNOVATIVE FLYING LLC | 1700 AIRPORT ROAD CONWAY, SC 29527 | (412)346-2110 |

# South Dakota

| Name | Address | Phone |
| --- | --- | --- |
| QUEST AVIATION INC | 47010 GREAT PLANES PLACE TEA, SD 57064 | (605)368-2841 |
| SOUTH DAKOTA STATE UNIVERSITY AVIATION PROGRAM | 4430 EAST HIGHWAY 12 ABERDEEN, SD 57401 | (605)225-1384 |
| SOUTH DAKOTA STATE UNIVERSITY AVIATION PROGRAM | 201 W 2ND ST SOUTH AIRPORT BROOKINGS, SD 57006 | (605)688-4366 |

# Tennessee

| Name | Address | Phone |
| --- | --- | --- |

| Name | Address | Phone |
|---|---|---|
| AIR VENTURE FLIGHT CENTER | 800 AIRPORT RD BOLIVAR, TN 38008 | (901)521-1068 |
| JAY AIR LLC DBA: 1. DOWNTOWN AVIATION LLC | 2787 NORTH SECOND STREET GENERAL DEWITT SPAIN AIRPORT MEMPHIS, TN 38127 | (901)353-9151 |
| JKG LLC DBA: 1. MURFREESBORO AVIATION | 1930 MEMORIAL BOULEVARD MURFREESBORO, TN 37129 | (615)494-1900 |
| MIDDLE TENNESSEE STATE UNIVERSITY | 1940 MEMORIAL BLVD. MURFREESBORO, TN 37129 | (615)890-5755 |
| TENNESSEE STATE UNIVERSITY | 3500 JOHN A MERRITT BLVD NASHVILLE, TN 37209 | (615)963-5378 |
| WINGS OF EAGLES LLC DBA: 1. JWN WINGS OF EAGLES 2. MQA WINGS OF EAGLES | 276 DOUG WARPOOLE RD SMYRNA, TN 37167 | (615)355-0033 |

# Texas

| Name | Address | Phone |
|---|---|---|

| | | |
|---|---|---|
| AEROSIM FLIGHT ACADEMY | ELLINGTON FIELD AIRPORT 12711 BLUME AVE HOUSTON, TX 77034 | (281)481-4700 |
| ALPHA TANGO FLYING SERVICES INC | 1331 NORTHERN BLVD SAN ANTONIO, TX 78216-4823 | (210)828-4480 |
| AMERICAN EUROCOPTER CORPORATION | 2701 FORUM DRIVE GRAND PRAIRIE, TX 75052 | (972)641-0000 |
| AMERICAN FLYERS INC | 4650 AIRPORT PARKWAY ADDISON AIRPORT ADDISON, TX 75001 | (214)765-9040 |
| AMERICAN FLYERS INC | 20803 STUEBNER AIRLINE ROAD BOX 32 SPRING, TX 77379 | (281)655-4500 |
| ANSON AIR LLC DBA: 1. ANSON AVIATION 2. SUGAR LAND AVIATION | 12888 HIGHWAY 6 SOUTH, SUITE 300 SUGAR LAND, TX 77478 | (281)242-2555 |
| AUSTIN ACADEMY OF AVIATION | 4309 EMMA BROWNING AVE. AUSTIN, TX 78719 | (512)385-2880 |
| AVIATION ACADEMY OF AMERICA INC | 1764 ENTRANCE DRIVE NEW BRAUNFELS, TX 78130 | (830)629-1700 |
| AVIATOR AIR CENTERS INC | 3122 GREAT SW PARKWAY GRAND PRAIRIE, TX | (972)988-8609 |

| 75052 | | |
|---|---|---|
| AVIATOUR INC<br>DBA:<br>1. CALIFORNIA FLIGHT CENTER | 730 FERRIS ROAD<br>SUITE 202<br>LANCASTER, TX 75146 | (877)837-2649 |
| BELL HELICOPTER TEXTRON<br>DBA:<br>1. BELL HELICOPTER TRAINING<br>ACADEMY | ALLIANCE AIRPORT<br>13901 AVIATION WAY<br>FORT WORTH, TX 76177 | (817)280-3971 |
| BRAZOS VALLEY FLIGHT<br>SERVICES | 1680 GEORGE BUSH<br>DRIVE WEST<br>STE. 2<br>COLLEGE STATION, TX<br>77845 | (979)260-6322 |
| CENTRAL TEXAS COLLEGE | SKYLARK FIELD<br>AIRPORT<br>1315 STONETREE DRIVE<br>KILLEEN, TX 76542-0000 | (254)699-5059 |
| DELTA AERONAUTICS INC<br>DBA:<br>1. DELTA-QUALIFLIGHT<br>AVIATION | 151 MEACHAM AIRPORT<br>CIRCLE<br>HANGER 4 NORTH<br>FORT WORTH, TX 76106 | (817)626-6300 |
| EPIC HELICOPTERS | 4201 N MAIN STREET<br>SUITE 109<br>FORT WORTH, TX 76106 | (817)625-1800 |
| GOLD STAR AVIATION | 200 COMMANDER RD.<br>HANGAR 2 NORTH, LOT<br>C<br>FORT WORTH, TX 76106 | (817)624-7320 |
| GRYPHON AVIATION INC<br>DBA:<br>1. TEXAS STATE AVIATION | 2049 AIRPORT DRIVE<br>SAN MARCOS, TX 78666 | (512)396-2212 |

| | | |
|---|---|---|
| HARVEY AND RIHN AVIATION INC | 101 AIRPORT BLVD LA PORTE, TX 77571 | (281)471-1675 |
| HELICOPTER EXPERTS INC | 29640 BULVERDE LANE BULVERDE, TX 78163 | (210)930-0125 |
| HUB CITY AVIATION INC | 6004 NORTH CEDAR AVE, SUITE #2 LUBBOCK, TX 79403-6800 | (806)687-1070 |
| LETOURNEAU UNIVERSITY | 200 AIRPARK ROAD EAST TEXAS REGIONAL AIRPORT LONGVIEW, TX 75603 | (903)233-4260 |
| LONGHORN HELICOPTERS INC | 5007 AIRPORT ROAD DENTON, TX 76207 | (940)387-2193 |
| MARCAIR INC | 11310 CLEVELAND GIBBS ROAD ROANOKE, TX 76262 | (817)430-0005 |
| MCCORVEY PREPARED PRECISION PRODUCTS L P DBA: 1. FLYING TIGERS | 11800 KIRK AVENUE, BUILDING W420 HOUSTON, TX 77034 | (281)464-6524 |
| MENAGERIE ENTERPRISES INC DBA: 1. MONARCH AIR | 4580 CLAIRE CHENNAULT ADDISON, TX 75001-5321 | (972)931-0345 |
| MIDLAND COLLEGE PROFESSIONAL PILOT PROGRAM | 901 VETERANS AIRPARK LN, HANGAR 10 MIDLAND, TX 79705 | (432)684-9800 |
| MOUNTAIN VIEW COLLEGE | 4849 W ILLINOIS AVE DALLAS, TX 75211 | (214)860-8774 |

| | | |
|---|---|---|
| PILOTS CHOICE AVIATION INC | 209 CORSAIR DRIVE GEORGETOWN, TX 78628 | (512)869-1759 |
| PORTER AVIATION SERVICES INC DBA: 1. SLIPSTREAM AVIATION | 5435 SATURN DRIVE DALLAS, TX 75237 | (817)658-5988 |
| PRAAT AIR SERVICES INC | 1909 JOE STEPHENS DR. HANGAR E24 WESLACO, TX 78596 | (956)975-2546 |
| PRO AIRCRAFT DBA: 1. PRO AIRCRAFT FLIGHT TRAINING | 137 AVIATOR DRIVE FORT WORTH, TX 76179-5424 | (817)439-3033 |
| PROFLIGHT AVIATION SERVICES LLC | 2080 AIRPORT DRIVE SAN MARCOS, TX 78666 | (210)860-4822 |
| SAN JACINTO COLLEGE | 8060 SPENCER HWY P O BOX 2007 PASADENA, TX 77505 | (281)478-2789 |
| SKY HELICOPTERS INC | 2559 S. JUPITER RD. GARLAND,, TX 75041 | (214)349-7000 |
| SKY SAFETY INC | 8603 MISSION RD. SAN ANTONIO, TX 78214 | (210)921-2504 |
| SKYMATES INC | 5080 SOUTH COLLINS STREET, STE 104 ARLINGTON, TX 76018 | (817)472-8307 |
| TEXAS STATE TECHNICAL COLLEGE | 3801 CAMPUS DR WACO, TX 76705 | (800)792-8784 |
| TEXAS STATE TECHNICAL COLLEGE WEST TEXAS | 2850 AIRPORT BLVD | (325)677-2601 |

| DBA:<br>1. TSTC AIR ACADEMY | ABILENE, TX 79602 | |
| --- | --- | --- |
| UNITED FLIGHT SYSTEMS | 20119A STUEBNER<br>AIRLINE<br>SPRING, TX 77379 | (281)376-0357 |
| US AVIATION GROUP LLC<br>DBA:<br>1. ALL AMERICAN HELICOPTER<br>2. US AVIATION ACADEMY | 4850 SPARTAN<br>DENTON MUNICIPAL<br>AIRPORT<br>DENTON, TX 76207 | (940)383-2484 |
| US AVIATION GROUP LLC<br>DBA:<br>1. US AVIATION ACADEMY -<br>HONDO | 900 VANDENBERG<br>ROAD<br>HONDO, TX 78861 | (210)246-6350 |
| US SPORT AIRCRAFT | 4700 AIRPORT<br>PARKWAY<br>ADDISON, TX 75001 | (972)735-9099 |
| VERACITY AVIATION LLC | 212 STEARMAN DR.<br>GEORGETOWN, TX<br>78628 | (512)868-5858 |
| VERACITY AVIATION LLC | 2475 RUDELOFF ROAD<br>SEGUIN, TX 78155 | (830)379-9800 |

# Utah

| Name | Address | Phone |
| --- | --- | --- |

| | | |
|---|---|---|
| BALLOON THE ROCKIES INC | 7749 NORTH WHILEAWAY PARK CITY, UT 84098 | (435)649-2517 |
| CORNERSTONE AVIATION INC | 3811 AIRPORT ROAD OGDEN, UT 84405 | (801)622-1222 |
| CORNERSTONE AVIATION INC | 2500 STATE STREET GRANITE TECHNICAL INSTITUTE SALT LAKE CITY, UT 84116 | (801)355-2244 |
| CORNERSTONE AVIATION INC | 337 NORTH 2370 WEST #130 SALT LAKE CITY, UT 84116 | (801)355-2244 |
| CORNERSTONE AVIATION INC | 250 WEST 3900 SOUTH SALT LAKE CITY, UT 84116 | (801)355-2244 |
| CORNERSTONE AVIATON INC | 9301 WIGHTS FORT ROAD JORDAN TECHNICAL CENTER WEST JORDAN,, UT 84088 | (801)355-2244 |
| LOGAN AIR SERVICES LLC DBA: 1. LEADING EDGE AVIATION | 7365 SOUTH 4450 WEST WEST JORDAN, UT 84084 | (801)858-0042 |
| MOUNTAIN RIDGE HELICOPTERS | 2500 NORTH 900 WEST FL-15 LOGAN, UT 84321 | (435)752-3828 |
| UHI INC DBA: 1. UNIVERSAL HELICOPTERS | 3421 MIKE JENSE PARKWAY PROVO, UT 84601 | (801)377-0077 |
| UPPER LIMIT AVIATION INC | 551 NORTH 2200 WEST SALT LAKE CITY, UT | (801)596-7722 |

| | 84116 | |
|---|---|---|
| UPPER LIMIT AVIATION INC | 9301 SOUTH WIGHT FORT ROAD WEST JORDAN, UT 84088 | (801)596-7722 |
| UPPER LIMIT AVIATION INC | 1560 SOUTH 200 EAST SALT LAKE CITY, UT 84115 | (801)596-7722 |
| UPPER LIMIT AVIATION INC | 2500 SOUTH STATE STREET SALT LAKE CITY, UT 84115 | (801)596-7722 |
| UPPER LIMIT AVIATION INC | 250 WEST 3900 SOUTH SALT LAKE CITY, UT 84107 | (801)957-5046 |
| UPPER LIMIT AVIATION INC | 619 N. 2360 W. SALT LAKE CITY, UT 84116 | (801)596-7722 |
| UTAH HELICOPTER INC | 7220 SOUTH 4450 WEST SUITE 203 WEST JORDAN, UT 84084 | (801)794-2480 |
| UTAH HELICOPTER INC | 4196 SOUTH AIRPORT ROAD ST. GEORGE, UT 84790 | (801)794-2480 |
| UTAH HELICOPTER INC | 2050 NORTH 300 WEST SPANISH FORK, UT 84660 | (801)794-2480 |
| UTAH STATE UNIVERSITY | 2500 NORTH 900 WEST LOGAN - CACHE COUNTY AIRPORT LOGAN, UT 84322-6000 | (435)797-1797 |

| | | |
|---|---|---|
| UTAH STATE UNIVERSITY | 6000 OLD MAIN HILL LOGAN, UT 84321 | (435)753-4287 |
| WESTMINSTER COLLEGE | 1840 SOUTH 1300 EAST SALT LAKE CITY, UT 84105 | (801)832-2141 |
| WESTMINSTER COLLEGE | 337 NORTH 2370 WEST, SUITE 221 SALT LAKE CITY, UT 84116 | (801)832-2910 |

# Vermont

| Name | Address | Phone |
|---|---|---|
| GREEN MOUNTAIN FLIGHT ACADEMY | 159 CATAMOUNT DRIVE MILTON, VT 05468 | (802)893-1003 |
| VERMONT FLIGHT ACADEMY | 355 VALLEY ROAD SOUTH BURLINGTON, VT 05403 | (802)863-5988 |

# Virginia

| Name | Address | Phone |
|---|---|---|
| AMERICAN HELICOPTERS INC | 10503 WAKEMAN DRIVE MANASSAS REGIONAL AIRPORT MANASSAS, VA 20110 | (703)368-9599 |
| AV ED FLIGHT SCHOOL INC | 1001 SYCOLIN RD LEESBURG, VA 20175 | (703)777-9252 |
| AVERETT UNIVERSITY | 427 AIRPORT DRIVE DANVILLE, VA 24540 | (434)791-5705 |

| | | |
|---|---|---|
| AVIATION ADVENTURES LLC | 1001 SYCOLIN ROAD SE LEESBURG, VA 20175 | (703)777-6030 |
| AVIATION ADVENTURES LLC | 10600 HARRY PARRISH BLVD SUITE 109 MANASSAS, VA 20110 | (703)530-7737 |
| DULLES AVIATION INC | 10501 OBSERVATION ROAD MANASSAS, VA 20110 | (703)361-2171 |
| HORIZON FLIGHT CENTER LLC | 2801 AIRPORT DRIVE CHESAPEAKE, VA 23323 | (757)421-9000 |
| JLS AVIATION LLC | 3380 SHANNON AIRPORT CIRCLE FREDERICKSBURG, VA 22405 | (540)374-1715 |
| LANGLEY AIR FORCE BASE AERO CLUB | LANGLEY AIR FORCE BASE AERO CLUB P.O. BOX 65686 LANGLEY AFB, VA 23665 | (757)766-1347 |
| LIBERTY UNIVERSITY | 310 HANGAR ROAD LYNCHBURG, VA 24502 | (434)582-2183 |
| NEW KENT AVIATION LLC | 6901 TERMINAL ROAD QUINTON, VA 23141 | (804)932-4220 |
| NORTH AMERICAN FLIGHT CENTER LLC | 970 AIRPORT RD BLDG AP210 LYNCHBURG, VA 24502 | (434)845-8769 |
| PREMIER FLIGHT ACADEMY LLC | 970 AIRPORT RD BLDG AP210 LYNCHBURG, VA 24502 | (434)477-5396 |

| RICK AIR FLIGHT SCHOOL | 902-D BLAND BOULEVARD NEWPORT NEWS, VA 23602 | (757)874-5727 |
|---|---|---|

# Washington

| Name | Address | Phone |
|---|---|---|
| NORTHWAY AVIATION | 10108 32ND AVE W BLDG C-3 EVERETT, WA 98204 | (425)742-7003 |
| AVIAN FLIGHT CENTER INC | 8900 STATE HWY. 3 SW SUITE 101 PORT ORCHARD, WA 98367 | (360)674-2111 |
| AVIATION TRAINING CENTER INC | 7170 PERIMETER ROAD SOUTH SEATTLE, WA 98108 | (206)768-1332 |
| BIG BEND COMMUNITY COLLEGE | AVIATION DEPARTMENT MOSES LAKE, WA 98837-3299 | (509)793-2241 |
| CENTRAL WASHINGTON UNIVERSITY | CENTRAL WASHINGTON UNIVERSITY AVIATION DEPARTMENT ELLENSBURG, WA 98926 | (509)963-2364 |
| CLASSIC HELICOPTER CORP | 8535 PERIMETER ROAD SOUTH BOEING FIELD SEATTLE, WA 98108 | (206)767-0515 |
| CLOVER PARK TECHNICAL COLLEGE | 17214 110TH AVE EAST PUYALLUP, WA 98374 | (253)583-8904 |
| CREST AIRPARK INC | 29300 179TH PLACE SE KENT, WA 98042 | (253)631-7100 |

| | | |
|---|---|---|
| GALVIN FLYING SERVICES INC | 7001 PERIMETER ROAD SOUTH SEATTLE, WA 98108 | (206)763-9706 |
| GREEN RIVER COMMUNITY COLLEGE | 12401 SE 320TH STREET AUBURN, WA 98092-3622 | (253)833-9111 |
| INLAND HELICOPTERS INC | 5505 E. RUTTER AVENUE SPOKANE, WA 99212 | (509)534-9114 |
| JDO SCHOOL OF AEROSPACE SCIENCES - SPOKANE | UND AEROSPACE FTC 3727 SO. DAVIDSON BLVD BLDG701 SPOKANE, WA 99219 | (509)462-0182 |
| JORGENSEN AIR SERVICE LLC | 7825 OLD HWY 99 SE TUMWATER, WA 98501 | (360)754-4043 |
| MIDSTATE AVIATION INC | 1101 BOWERS ROAD ELLENSBURG, WA 98926 | (509)962-7850 |
| MOODY BIBLE INSTITUTE OF CHICAGO DBA: 1. MOODY AVIATION | 6719 E. RUTTER AVE. SPOKANE, WA 99212 | (509)535-4051 |
| MORCOM AVIATION SERVICES INC DBA: 1. REGAL AIR | 10100 30TH AVE. W, BLDG C-51 EVERETT, WA 98204 | (425)353-9123 |
| PAVCO INC | 1110 26TH AVENUE NW GIG HARBOR, WA 98335 | (253)851-5577 |
| RAINIER FLIGHT SERVICE | 790 W. PERIMETER RD. RENTON, WA 98057 | (425)610-6293 |
| SAFETY IN MOTION FLIGHT CENTER INC | 16911 103RD AVE E, #102 | (253)840-5758 |

| DBA: 1. SIM FLIGHT CENTER | PUYALLUP, WA 98374 | |
|---|---|---|
| SNOHOMISH FLYING SERVICE INC | 9900 AIRPORT WAY HARVEY FIELD SNOHOMISH, WA 98296-8218 | (360)568-1541 |

# West Virginia

| Name | Address | Phone |
|---|---|---|
| AERO-SMITH INC | 214 AVIATION WAY MARTINSBURG, WV 25405 | (304)262-3739 |
| ROBERT C BYRD NATIONAL AEROSPACE EDUCATION CENTER | 1050 E. BENEDUM INDUSTRIAL DRIVE BRIDGEPORT, WV 26330 | (304)842-8300 |

# Wisconsin

| Name | Address | Phone |
|---|---|---|
| GATEWAY TECHNICAL COLLEGE | 3520 30TH AVENUE KENOSHA, WI 53144-1690 | (262)564-3218 |
| JET AIR GROUP INC DBA: 1. FRONTLINE AVIATION | 1921 AIRPORT DRIVE GREEN BAY, WI 54313 | (920)497-4900 |
| WISCONSIN AVIATION INC | 3606 CORBEN COURT MADISON, WI 53703 | (608)268-5000 |
| WISCONSIN AVIATION INC | DODGE COUNTY AIRPORT N6491 STATE ROAD 26 JUNEAU, WI 53039-1329 | (920)306-2402 |

| | | |
|---|---|---|
| WISCONSIN AVIATION INC | WATERTOWN MUNICIPAL AIRPORT<br>1741 RIVER DRIVE<br>WATERTOWN, WI 53094 | (920)261-4567 |

# Wyoming

| Name | Address | Phone |
|---|---|---|
| CROSSWIND AVIATION INC | NATRONA COUNTY AIRPORT<br>7548 FULLER STREET<br>CASPER, WY 82604 | (307)472-4359 |
| PRAIRIE AVIATION INC | 3001 DUGGLEBY DRIVE<br>PO BOX 1570<br>CODY, WY 82414 | (307)899-3409 |
| WINGS OF WYOMING INC | 3803 EVANS AVENUE<br>CHEYENNE, WY 82001 | (307)778-3050 |

# ABOUT THE AUTHOR

Gregory Youngs is a professional pilot, entrepreneur and author. He is currently living in Texas with his wife and two children. His aviation career has included banner towing, glider towing, crop dusting, charter, airline and corporate flying.

More career information is available at
www.howtobeanairlinepilot.com

CPSIA information can be obtained at www.ICGtesting.com
Printed in the USA
LVOW10s0513121215

466395LV00030B/1432/P

9 781496 003201